A Hurting Sport

Books by Thomas Hauser

General Non-Fiction
Missing
The Trial of Patrolman Thomas Shea
For Our Children (with Frank Macchiarola)
The Family Legal Companion
Final Warning: The Legacy of Chernobyl (with Dr. Robert Gale)
Arnold Palmer: A Personal Journey
Confronting America's Moral Crisis (with Frank Macchiarola)
Healing: A Journal of Tolerance and Understanding
With This Ring (with Frank Macchiarola)
Thomas Hauser on Sports
Reflections

Boxing Non-Fiction
The Black Lights: Inside the World of Professional Boxing
Muhammad Ali: His Life and Times
Muhammad Ali: Memories
Muhammad Ali: In Perspective
Muhammad Ali & Company
A Beautiful Sickness
A Year At The Fights
Brutal Artistry
The View From Ringside
Chaos, Corruption, Courage, and Glory
The Lost Legacy of Muhammad Ali
I Don't Believe It, But It's True
Knockout (with Vikki LaMotta)
The Greatest Sport of All
The Boxing Scene
An Unforgiving Sport
Boxing Is . . .
Box: The Face of Boxing
The Legend of Muhammad Ali (with Bart Barry)
Winks and Daggers
And the New . . .
Straight Writes and Jabs
Thomas Hauser on Boxing
A Hurting Sport

Fiction
Ashworth & Palmer
Agatha's Friends
The Beethoven Conspiracy
Hanneman's War
The Fantasy
Dear Hannah
The Hawthorne Group
Mark Twain Remembers
Finding The Princess
Waiting For Carver Boyd
The Final Recollections of Charles Dickens
The Baker's Tale

For Children
Martin Bear & Friends

A Hurting Sport

An Inside Look at Another Year in Boxing

Thomas Hauser

The University of Arkansas Press
Fayetteville
2015

ISBN: 978-1-55728-683-3
e-ISBN: 978-1-61075-572-6

19   18   17   16   15   5   4   3   2   1

∞The paper used in this publication meets the minimum requirements of the
American National Standard for Permanence of Paper for Printed Library
Materials Z39.48-1984.

Library of Congress Control Number: 2015938419

For Peter Nelson and Ray Stallone

Contents

Fighters and Fights

Behind the Scenes at Pacquiao–Bradley 2   3

Sergio Martinez vs. Miguel Cotto   16

Chris Algieri: An Unlikely Champion   24

Boyd Melson: An Atypical Fighter   29

GGG = WOW   35

New York Notes   39

Jermain Taylor's "Comeback"   47

Hopkins-Kovalev: A Legacy Fight   51

A Look Back at Hopkins-Kovalev   56

Larry Holmes at Ecco   64

Non-Combatants

Remembering Paul Hoggatt   69

Don Turner: Opinions and Memories   76

John Duddy: Actor   79

Curiosities

"I'm Going Down"   85

David Diamante at Pamplona   89

Tina and Manny Redux   92

HBO's "Delta Force"   95

Fistic Nuggets   98

Issues and Answers

Floyd Mayweather, Donald Sterling, and TMZ   111

What Is Al Haymon Planning?   116

Instant Video Review and Boxing   126

Fistic Notes   131

The SCP Summer Premier Auction   149

Mayweather and Pacquiao vs. the Modern 135-Pound Greats   153

100 Days: The New York Times and Boxing   158
Floyd Mayweather and Ray Rice   166
Literary Notes   171
In Memoriam   182
Floyd Mayweather, Showtime, and the Nevada State Athletic
        Commission   196

Author's Note

A Hurting Sport contains the articles about professional boxing that I authored in 2014. The articles I wrote about the sweet science prior to that date have been published in *Muhammad Ali & Company*; *A Beautiful Sickness*; *A Year at the Fights*; *The View From Ringside*; *Chaos, Corruption, Courage, and Glory*; *The Lost Legacy of Muhammad Ali*; *I Don't Believe It, But It's True*; *The Greatest Sport of All*, *The Boxing Scene*, *An Unforgiving Sport*; *Boxing Is*; *Winks and Daggers*; *And the New*; *Straight Writes and Jabs*; and *Thomas Hauser on Boxing*.

Fighters and Fights

Manny Pacquiao and Tim Bradley stand for the proposition that nice guys can finish first.

Behind the Scenes at Pacquiao-Bradley 2

Shortly after one o'clock on the afternoon of Thursday, April 10, Manny Pacquiao concluded a series of satellite interviews that originated in Section 118 of the MGM Grand Garden Arena in Las Vegas. The interviews were designed to promote his April 12, 2014, fight against Tim Bradley, and everything had gone according to plan.

"My advantage is that I'm quicker than him and punch harder than him," Pacquiao told one interviewer.

When asked about being knocked out by Juan Manuel Marquez, Manny responded, "Sometimes these things happen. That is boxing."

An interviewer for Sky TV posed the all-but-obligatory question of whether or not Pacquiao would fight Floyd Mayweather.

"I'm happy for that fight," Manny said. "If not in boxing, maybe we can play one-on-one in basketball."

As for his musical talents, Pacquiao acknowledged, "I can sing, but my voice is really not that good. The fans like my singing because of what I've done in boxing."

At one point, Manny noted, "Sportsmanship is very important to me because it is my way of displaying respect to the sport of boxing, to my opponent, and to the fans."

After the interviews ended, Pacquiao was leaving Section 118 when a voice from across the arena shouted out loud and clear: "Manny, we love you. Manny, we love you. Manny! Manny!"

Pacquiao turned to acknowledge the fan, one of many who follow him wherever he goes. Then his face broke into a broad smile. The man shouting was Tim Bradley.

Manny waved, Tim waved back. In two days, they would try to beat each other senseless in a boxing ring. But for now, there was fondness between them.

Welcome to Pacquiao-Bradley 2, featuring two elite fighters who carried themselves with dignity and grace throughout the promotion with no lapse of decorum by either man.

Pacquiao's saga is well known. In an era of phony championship belts and unremitting hype, he has been a legitimate champion and also a true peoples' champion. The eleven-month period between December 6, 2008, and November 14, 2009, when he demolished Oscar De La Hoya, Ricky Hatton, and Miguel Cotto were his peak years in terms of ring performance and adulation.

That was a while ago.

Tim Bradley believes in himself and epitomizes Cus D'Amato's maxim: "When two fighters meet in the ring, the fighter with the greater will prevails every time unless his opponent's skills are so superior that the opponent's will is never tested."

Most elite athletes are overachievers. Bradley comes as close to getting 100 percent out of his potential as anyone in boxing. He's a more sophisticated fighter than many people give him credit for. He's not just about coming forward, applying pressure, and throwing punches. He has a good boxing brain and knows how to use it. But he isn't particularly fast, nor does he hit particularly hard. The keys to his success are his physical strength and iron will.

"I'm not the most talented fighter in the division," Tim acknowledges. "Not at all. There are guys with better skills and better physical gifts than I have. Where I separate myself from other fighters is my determination. I wear the other guy down. That's what it is; hard work and determination. I work my butt off. I come ready every time. People keep saying that I don't hit that hard, that I don't box that well. But I keep winning, don't I?"

Before each fight, Bradley promises himself that his opponent will remember him for the rest of his life. Marvin Hagler is his favorite fighter. Blue-collar work ethic, shaved head, overshadowed by boxing's glamour boys.

Pacquiao and Bradley met in the ring for the first time on June 9, 2012. During that bout, Tim suffered strained ligaments in his left foot and a badly swollen right ankle. He was rolled into the post-fight press conference in a wheelchair.

"Both of my feet were hurt in that fight," he recalls. "And I had a lion in front of me. All I could do was take it round by round. And it wasn't enough to survive each round. I had to win them."

Bradley, as the world knows, prevailed on a split decision. A firestorm of protest followed.

In the aftermath of the bout, Pacquiao was an exemplary sportsman. "I'm a fighter," Manny said. "My job is to fight in the ring. I don't judge the fights. This is sport. You're on the winner's side sometimes. Sometimes you're on the loser's side. If you don't want to lose, don't fight."

But others were less gracious. The beating that Bradley took outside the ring was worse than the punishment he took in it.

"After the fight," Tim remembers, "they announced that I was the winner. I was on top of the world, and then the world caved in on me. It should have been the happiest time of my life, and I wound up in the darkest place I've ever been in. I thought the fight was close. I thought the decision could have gone either way. You prepare your entire life to get to a certain point; you get there; and then it all gets taken away. I was attacked in the media. People were stopping me on the street, saying things like, 'You didn't win that fight; you should give the belt back; you should be ashamed of yourself; you're not a real champion.' I got death threats. I turned off my phone. All I did was do my job the best way I could, and it was like I stole something from the world."

"It was bad," says Joel Diaz, who has trained Bradley for the fighter's entire career. "Tim was all right with people criticizing the decision, but the personal attacks really hurt. Tim is a proud man, and it was hard for him to walk tall anywhere."

In Pacquiao's next fight, he suffered a one-punch knockout loss at the hands of Juan Manuel Marquez. Eleven months later, he rebounded to decision Brandon Rios. Meanwhile, Bradley edged Ruslan Provodnikov in a thriller and outboxed Marquez en route to another split-decision triumph.

That set the stage for the April 12 rematch at the MGM Grand in Las Vegas. Bradley was the reigning champion, but Pacquiao was the engine driving the economics of the fight. The event was labeled "Pacquiao-Bradley 2", and Manny was guaranteed a $20 million purse ($6 million less than for their initial encounter). Tim was promised $6 million (one million more than the first time around).

Each fighter felt that there was unfinished business between them.

"There is a big question mark on our first fight," Pacquiao said at a February 6 press conference in New York. "This time, we will answer that question."

"The whole Pacquiao situation still bothers me," Bradley added. "So on April 12, I'm going to clean that up."

Fight week had a strange feel to it. The Pacquiao-Bradley rematch hadn't taken place earlier because neither HBO nor Top Rank (which promoted both fighters) thought it would sell well. But after Marquez starched Pacquiao and Bradley beat Marquez, the possibility of beating Tim loomed as a more impressive credential for Manny. Also, as part of a deal to secure the fight, Bradley agreed to a two-year extension of his promotional contract, which was due to expire in December 2014.

That said; the promotion was struggling a bit.

Elite fighters have a glow, an aura around them. Pacquiao in his prime was electrifying. But in recent years, the Pacquiao super nova has dimmed.

In the days leading up to Pacquiao-Bradley 2, the narrative was no longer about Manny's Magical Adventure. The media no longer waited in heightened anticipation for his arrival at publicity events. The fighter himself seemed to have a bit of "Pacquiao fatigue." Certainly, he was aware of the talk that his career was nearing an end.

Again and again during fight week, Manny told interviewers, "My time in boxing is not yet done. I want to prove that my journey in boxing will continue."

There was the mandatory appearance by Pacquiao on *Jimmy Kimmel Live* and all of the ritual hype. But pay-per-view sales were tracking poorly, an estimated 650,000 to 700,000 buys (down from 875,000 for the first Pacquiao-Bradley fight). Ticket sales were respectable, but there wouldn't be a sellout.

It was Bradley who generated much of the energy in the media center. Tim is inherently likable with an exuberance for life and a smile that lights up a room when he enters. Insofar as his status as a role model is concerned, he and his wife, Monica, appear to have a loving stable marriage. When Bradley takes his children to school in the morning, it's not a designed photo op for television cameras. There's no bimbo girlfriend, no charge of domestic violence, no conspicuous spending. The thought of Tim blowing twenty thousand dollars in a strip club is ludicrous.

Bradley loves challenges. "I'm looking forward to the fight," he told the media. "It will be fun."

Reflecting on his football-playing days, Tim opined, "Boxing is more fun than playing quarterback. I like it better where, if someone hits me, I can hit him back."

Defending the judges' decision in Pacquiao-Bradley I, Tim told an interviewer, "Everybody has an opinion. That means I have an opinion too. Manny Pacquiao is one of the best fighters ever to lace on a pair of gloves. I'm a big fan of Manny Pacquiao. But I beat him."

Then the interviewer stated proudly that he was rooting for Pacquiao, and Bradley responded, "If you're a Pacquiao fan; hey, Manny is a good dude. I respect the person he is and I respect what he has done for the sport. I have no problem with anyone who roots for him."

That left the trashtalking to Bob Arum, who spent much of the week denouncing the host site and the MGM Grand's president of entertainment, Richard Sturm.

Arum was appropriately angry that the hotel-casino was festooned with advertising for the May 3 fight between Floyd Mayweather and Marcos Maidana to the detriment of his own promotion. Introducing Sturm at the final pre-fight press conference on Wednesday, he referenced the executive as "the president of hanging posters and decorations for the wrong fight."

Then, at the end of the press conference, Arum went further, declaring, "I know the Venetian [which had hosted Pacquiao's previous fight in Macau] would never make a mistake like this. They would know what fight was scheduled in three or four days, and they wouldn't have a 12-to-1 fight all over the building that's going to take place three weeks from Saturday. That's why one company makes a billion dollars a quarter and the other hustles to pay its debt."

The following day, Arum elaborated on that theme, telling reporters, "There are two companies which are the leading American companies in gaming, and it's for a reason. It's because they're smarter than these guys, and they know what they're doing. First is the Venetian-Sands company and then there is the Wynn. Pick up a paper and look at where the stock of each company is going. Then tell me who has smarter people. Is it luck? I don't think so. If one company is making so much more than the other company and doesn't have financial problems because they borrowed too much money, it's not luck. It's because they're smarter and conduct themselves better. This company really has a serious management problem."

Thereafter, in various interviews, Arum called Sturm "a horse's ass . . . totally clueless . . . a moron . . . a brain-dead moron," and added, "He doesn't have a fucking clue what the fuck he's doing."

On Friday, the promoter proclaimed, "They [the MGM Grand] did something that I believe is an absolutely horrendous thing to do. It shows tremendous disrespect for the Filipino people, who are such nice people. If I were Filipino, I would never patronize an MGM Hotel again."

Then, as a helpful guide to Filipino high rollers who might have been offended by the slight, Arum listed all of the MGM Grand properties that they might want to avoid in the future.

Meanwhile, the odds had settled on Pacquiao as a 9-to-5 favorite, down from 4 to 1 in the first Pacquiao-Bradley encounter.

Bradley has never been thought of as a big puncher. His ledger shows a meager twelve knockouts, with only one in the past seven years. Pacquiao, by contrast, has thirty-eight career KOs. But Manny's record is devoid of stoppages since his 2009 demolition of Miguel Cotto.

That led Bradley to declare, "Manny is still sensational physically, but I don't think the fire is there anymore. He's not the same fighter he used to be. He's still a tremendous fighter. But the killer instinct, the hunger, is gone and it won't come back again. Manny fights for the money. I have the hunger to win. I just feel that his heart isn't in it anymore."

Were Bradley's comments about Pacquiao no longer having "killer instinct" designed to undermine Manny's confidence? Or perhaps to goad him into fighting recklessly?

"Neither," Tim answered. "I'm simply stating a fact."

Team Pacquiao didn't entirely disagree with Bradley's thoughts. Trainer Freddie Roach acknowledged, "Recently, Manny has felt it was enough to just win his fights. He didn't want to hurt his opponent more than he had to. I've had a lot of talks with him about that, and I'm sure it's not going to happen again. When Bradley told Manny that he'd lost the killer instinct, frankly, Manny got pissed off. He thought it was disrespectful."

"Sometimes I'm too nice to my opponent," Pacquiao added. "I have been happy winning on points because it is winning. But the fans want to see that hunger from me, and I'm always concerned about the fans and their satisfaction. So I'm going to fight this fight to show that I still have that hunger and that killer instinct."

But there were questions as to whether, intent aside, Pacquiao still had the strength and physical stamina to close the show against an elite opponent.

"To me, it's not about killer instinct," Joel Diaz noted. "I don't think Pacquiao is being compassionate. I don't think he can finish anymore. Look at what happened when he fought Marquez in their third fight. The judges scored it for Pacquiao, but a lot of people thought Marquez should have won. Everyone knew it was close. And Pacquiao couldn't come on strong late. Pacquiao is getting older. He's not the fighter he used to be in the second half of his fights."

Bradley understood that there are no sure things in boxing. "I may lose this fight," he said in a teleconference call. "You never know. Things happen in the ring when you least expect it. It only takes one punch to end the night." But as Pacquiao-Bradley 2 approached, Tim was confident, saying, "I'm a more mature fighter now than I was two years ago. I'm better at getting in and out on guys and controlling the distance between us, which I showed in the Marquez fight. I'm a better fighter now than I was the first time Pacquiao and I fought. And Manny can't say that."

"This is the first time I've fought the same guy twice," Bradley continued. "And I think it's an advantage for me. The first time we fought, I didn't know how much intensity Manny brought to the ring. Omigod! He throws so many feints and closes the distance so fast and punches from all angles. He always keeps you guessing when he's going to come in and out. Now I know what to expect. I was able to make adjustments in the first fight, and Manny had problems with me when I was moving. I'm excited; I'm happy. On Saturday night, I'll get to show what I can do on the biggest stage possible. I know there are people who say I can't hurt him. If Manny feels that way, let him come in reckless and see what happens."

And there was another factor to consider. In his first fight against Pacquiao, Bradley had done something stupid. For the only time in his career, he'd entered the ring without socks because he'd once heard Mike Tyson say that going sockless helped him grip the canvas and increase the leverage on his punches. Bradley had trained sockless in the gym for

that fight. But the canvas in the ring on fight night was different from
the gym canvas. And the demands on fight night are different from the
demands of sparring. In the early going against Pacquiao, Tim had suffered ligament damage in his left foot and sprained his right ankle.

"With two good feet, I'll be able to move quicker this time and set
down harder on my punches," Bradley promised. "With two good feet,
I can adjust my footwork to deal with whatever Pacquiao brings to the
table. Pain-free is another dimension, and I'll be pain-free this time."

Indeed, the main concern in Bradley's camp was that the judges
might overcompensate for the perceived injustice of the scoring in
Pacquiao-Bradley 1 and, fearing ridicule, have a default setting on close
rounds in favor of Manny.

"We know the judges will have a lot of weight on their backs," Joel
Diaz noted. "The stage was set for Tim to lose the first fight, and it didn't
happen. Now the stage is set for Tim to lose again. If the fight goes the
distance and it's close, the judges will give it to Pacquiao. All I ask is for
the judges to be fair. If Tim wins, give him the win. If Pacquiao wins,
give him the win."

Meanwhile, as the clock to fight night ticked down, it seemed as
though Bradley had more enthusiasm for the battle than Pacquiao did.

"I got something to prove," Tim declared. "I got something to prove
to the media; I got something to prove to the fans; I got something
to prove to everyone who says I didn't win the first fight. This fight is
redemption for me. I feel deep in my heart that I won the first fight and
I didn't get any credit. I'm going to beat Manny Pacquiao again. And this
time, I want the credit for it."

Team Pacquiao, of course, had a different view.

"Bradley is a very good fighter," trainer Freddie Roach said. "He's
tough and resilient. He takes good shots. He has a good chin. He has
determination and a lot of heart. When you hit him, he fights back."

"But I don't think Bradley has all the abilities that Manny has,"
Roach continued. "He's not as fast. He doesn't punch as hard. When
Manny is on his toes and uses his footspeed, he closes the distance better
than any fighter in the world. Once you put Bradley on the ropes, his
chin goes up in the air, he opens up, and he punches wild. When that
happens, Manny can beat him down the middle. Once the scores have

been announced and you've lost a fight, there's nothing you can do about it except say, 'We'll get him next time.' I think Manny beat this guy once, and I think he'll beat him again."

Pacquiao agreed with his mentor.

"I am impressed with what Bradley has done since our fight," Manny acknowledged. "His style is hard to explain. He is not easy to beat. But I am still faster than Bradley and I still punch harder than Bradley. He says that he wants to see my killer instinct, so he will see it."

★ ★ ★

Tim Bradley arrived in dressing room #1 at the MGM Grand Garden Arena at 6:00 pm on Saturday night. He was wearing a black Nike track suit with a white Team Bradley logo and black Nike shoes with white trim. Tim's father (known as "Big Ray"), Joel Diaz, assistant trainer Samuel Jackson, conditioning coach James Rougely, and attorney Gaby Penagaricano were with him.

Bradley sat on a cushioned metal chair and rested his feet on another chair in front of him. HBO production coordinator Tami Cotel entered the room and asked if Tim would weigh-in on HBO's fight-night scale. Bradley complied. One day earlier, he'd tipped the official scale at 145 ½ pounds. Now he weighed 152. Minutes earlier, Pacquiao (who'd weighed in officially at 145) had registered 151 pounds.

Brief dressing-room interviews with Max Kellerman and Bernardo Osuna followed. Then Tim sat back on the chair and closed his eyes, envisioning the battle ahead. His family's financial future, his physical well-being, and his legacy as a fighter were all at risk. He was as well prepared as he could be. But in all likelihood, so was Pacquiao.

At 6:25, Freddie Roach came into the room to watch Bradley's hands being wrapped. Tim took off his wedding ring and handed it to his father for safekeeping. Joel Diaz began taping. Roach's own hands were shaking visibly, a symptom of his Parkinson's condition. Big Ray offered him a chair. Roach gestured "no thank you."

No one spoke. At 6:40, the taping was done. Tim took off his jacket and shadow-boxed for ten minutes, stopping twice to sip water from a bottle that his father was holding. Then he sat down again.

Bradley gets his game face on earlier than most fighters. The next few hours would be about fighting, not charm school. The look on his face said, "Don't fuck with me." He was summoning up an attitude.

Joel Diaz went next door to watch Roach wrap Pacquiao's hands.

Tim stayed on the chair—sometimes with his eyes closed, sometimes open; sometimes with his head up, sometimes down—playing different fight sequences through in his mind.

If I do this, Pacquiao will do that. If Pacquiao does that, what do I do next?

The mood in the dressing room was intense. There were no attempts at levity, no smiles, no upbeat conversation. Few words were spoken.

At 7:10, Big Ray spread two towels side-by-side on the floor. Tim lay down and began a series of stretching exercises; first on his own, then with his father's assistance. The exercises grew progressively more rigorous. At 7:40, Big Ray picked up the towels and Tim shadow-boxed again.

Referee Kenny Bayless entered and gave the fighter his pre-fight instructions.

After Bayless left, Tim resumed shadow-boxing.

Big Ray stepped in front of his son with a folded-up towel in each hand, assumed a southpaw stance to emulate Pacquiao, and aimed punches at his son. "Don't let him get lower than you," he cautioned.

"Put it together any way you want," Diaz counseled. "You're not a one-dimensional fighter."

At eight o'clock, Tim sat, once again staring silently ahead.

Big Ray, Diaz, and Samuel Jackson took on the role of a Greek chorus, voicing thoughts one at a time.

"Fast like lightning."

"Stay loose."

"Control the pace. Make him do things he doesn't want to do, and he'll get tired."

"Don't be a gentleman. Rip his ass up on the inside."

The voices were complementing, not competing with, each other.

"It ain't about strength. It's about knowledge."

"That right hand will get him every time."

"Fight like a cat."

"Fight smart."

Big Ray slammed the palm of his hand down hard on the table beside him.

"Do not be on the ropes," he said. "Do not be on the ropes. You're in deep shit if you're on the ropes."

Diaz gloved Tim up.

More shadow-boxing.

Again, the Greek chorus.

"That's the way. Snap those punches."

"On the inside, keep both hands up by your head."

"Watch for his right hook on the inside."

"It's your night, baby. It's your night."

Tim sat.

"I'm excited," he said.

Then he fell silent, his face registering a range of emotions.

The Greek chorus continued to sound in his ears.

"Right hand to the body. Hook to the body. Tear that body up."

"If he gets under you, come up with the uppercut."

"The conditioning is there. He won't be able to deal with the pace."

"Control him. Don't let him control you."

"Patience is a virtue. Take your time. If it goes twelve, amen."

More shadow-boxing.

"We're happy, man; we're happy. Have fun"

"Fight smart."

"You're the real deal, babe."

Bradley began hitting the pads with Joel Diaz.

"Right over the top," Diaz instructed. "Beautiful. You got twelve rounds, twelve fuckin' rounds to time that punch. You're the champion. You're the boss. You're the big dog. You're the man."

The padwork ended.

Earlier in the week, Diaz had said, "In this sport, the most important thing is to be a professional at all times, in the ring and out of it." Now he told the men around him, "We're a team. Whatever happens in the ring tonight, we keep our composure."

Pacquiao could be seen on a television monitor at the far end of the room, leaving his dressing room and walking to the ring.

"It's fun time, baby," Bradley said.

Then the members of Team Bradley joined hands in a circle and Tim led them in prayer. He asked for the strength to prevail in the battle ahead. He asked that both he and Pacquiao emerge in good health. And he closed with a final thought for the Creator.

"Love you, man."

★ ★ ★

The fight itself was heartbreak for Bradley. After a tactical first round, the combatants exchanged in the second stanza with Pacquiao getting the better of the action. In round three, Manny scored big early and maintained his edge with speed and angles. Then Bradley found a home for his right hand, buzzed Pacquiao with a hard right up top, and took rounds four and five.

At that point, Bradley seemed to be where he wanted to be in the fight. Two of the judges (Michael Pernick and Craig Metcalfe) had him leading three rounds to two, while Glenn Trowbridge's card was the reverse. Tim's strategy from day one had been premised on the idea that the second half of the fight would belong to him.

But the unthinkable was happening. After round three, Bradley had returned to his corner and told Joel Diaz, "I pulled a muscle in my calf."

Now Tim's gastrocnemius muscle was tearing apart.

"You're losing your rhythm," Diaz told his charge after round six. "What the fuck is wrong?"

"I'm hurting," Tim answered.

The rest of the fight belonged to Pacquiao. Except for a right hand to the body that hurt Manny visibly in round seven, Bradley couldn't do much more than survive. He was an impaired fighter. And round by round, the injury was getting worse.

Tim backed into corners, beckoned Manny in, and swung for the fences with wild right hands up top. The constant grinding aggression characteristic of his style was absent. It was an inexplicable strategy unless one knew the truth.

The final scoring of the judges was anti-climactic: 118–110, 116–112, 116–112 for Pacquiao.

Monica Bradley was waiting for her husband when Tim returned to the dressing room after the fight. Their fourteen-year-old son, Robert, and Tim's mother were with her.

A large lump was visible on the back of Bradley's right calf. He was limping badly.

"What's up, baby?" Tim asked as he hugged Monica.

Then father and son embraced. "Some you lose; some you win," Tim said. "A champion has to accept defeat when it comes. I tried my best."

A kiss for Kathy Bradley was next. "I love you," Tim told his mother.

Joel Diaz took out his cellphone and began snapping photos of the lump on Bradley's calf.

A commission doctor came in and examined the injury.

"I don't want to go to the emergency room," Tim told the doctor. "And no wheelchair. I'm walking out on my own tonight."

Two days later, the injury was fully diagnosed. Bradley will be wearing a moon boot for the next month.

The muscle tear was frustrating given its impact on the fight and the role of the fight in Bradley's life. But overall, fate has been kind to Tim. In his three fights prior to this one (against Pacquiao, Provodnikov, and Marquez), he won decisions that could have gone the other way.

A fighter's first loss is particularly hard to accept, but Tim took it in stride. "I lost to one of the best fighters in the world," he told those gathered around him. "Pacquiao was on his game tonight. I did the best I could. I knew I was behind on points, so I went for the knockout with what I had. I'm a fighter. I'll be back. I'd like to fight him again, but he probably won't want to."

Meanwhile, in the dressing room next door, Team Pacquiao was celebrating. But their joy was tempered by a deep cut over the left eye that Manny suffered after an accidental clash of heads in the final round. Thirty-five stitches would be needed to close the gash.

Pacquiao's journey in boxing will continue.

So will Bradley's.

Sergio Martinez had a good championship run: seven victories in an impressive four-year reign. But in boxing, as in the rest of life, all good things must end.

Sergio Martinez vs. Miguel Cotto

At 9:15 on the night of June 7, 2014, Sergio Martinez entered dressing room #5 at Madison Square Garden with trainer Pablo Sarmiento, cutman Roger Anderson, and physical therapist Raquel Bordons. Cornerman Russ Anber and Nathan Lewkowicz (the son of promoter Sampson Lewkowicz) followed. The room was small and angularly shaped with brown industrial carpet and cream-colored cinderblock walls. Two doors down the corridor, Miguel Cotto was ensconced in dressing room #3.

In two-and-a-half hours, Martinez and Cotto would battle for the middleweight championship of the world. Sergio was the defending champion, but his dressing room was one-third the size of Miguel's. Other slights had cut deeper.

The fight and all promotional material for it had been styled "Cotto-Martinez" rather than the other way around. "It bothers me," Sergio admitted, "because it's disrespectful to the history and traditions of boxing. But Cotto said there would be no fight if his name wasn't first on the posters. I can imagine that, on June 7, he will ask for rose petals to be thrown at his feet or he won't walk to the ring."

More significantly, the finances of the fight were weighted in the challenger's favor. Cotto and Top Rank (Miguel's promoter) had retained Puerto Rican television rights off the top. The first $15,000,000 in net revenue after that would be split 55 percent to Cotto and Top Rank, 45 percent to Martinez and his promoters (DiBella Entertainment and Sampson Promotions). Thereafter, the split would increase to 60–40.

To Cotto, that was fair and logical. "Two times in my career—when I fought Pacquiao and when I fought Mayweather—I was the champion but I was the B-side," Miguel noted. "I understood my position. Sergio Martinez is a great fighter, but boxing is a business. For this fight, I am the one who sells the tickets."

A fighter's dressing room is a sheltered world in the hours before a big fight. In Sergio's case, the mood is constant from bout to bout;

relaxed and low-key until the final minutes when smiles evaporate.

Some fighters are intimidated by the atmosphere of a big fight. Martinez thrives on it. He loves the spotlight. His 2012 bout against Julio Cesar Chavez Jr had been more personal for him than this one because of the backroom dealing that led to his championship being temporarily taken from him. But he'd reclaimed the throne in front of a raucous crowd of Chavez partisans. Now he was eager to perform on an even bigger stage.

Referee Mike Griffin came into the dressing room and gave Martinez his pre-fight instructions. Russ Anber wrapped Sergio's hands. Martinez put on his shoes and trunks and shadow-boxed briefly. Then he pulled a protective latex sleeve up over each knee. "A precaution," he explained. "Not a necessity."

A precaution deemed advisable because of the knee surgery and rehabilitation that Martinez underwent last year.

Pablo Sarmiento gloved Sergio up. Earlier in the evening, New York State Athletic Commission inspector Ernie Morales had initialed Martinez's handwraps. Now Sue Etkin (the other inspector assigned to Sergio) wrote "Sue" on the tape covering the lace on each glove.

Martinez hit the pads with Sarmiento.

Music played. "Out of Control," sung by the group You Aren't Going to Like This. The same song, again and again.

There was anticipation in Sergio's eyes. Madison Square Garden . . . The middleweight championship of the world . . . A screaming bloodlust crowd of 21,090 waited. For Muhammad Ali, boxing was a sport. Joe Frazier treated it as combat. In Martinez's mind, he was preparing for a sporting competition. Two doors down the corridor, Miguel Cotto was preparing for combat.

Like most fighters, Martinez comes from a hard world. He's a thoughtful intelligent man, sometimes philosophical. Growing up in the slums of Buenos Aires, he didn't know what "dinner" was. The family didn't sit down together at an appointed hour. When food came into the home, they ate it.

"When you are very small, a child, you don't know that you're poor," Sergio says, reflecting back on that time. "Even though you're hungry and cold, if you have the love of your parents, you're happy with what you have because you're used to that life and it's all you know. Then you become an adolescent. You start to realize what you don't have and begin to think about how to get what you want. You can work hard or you can take the shorter path and turn to crime. If you have good parents, it makes a big difference in deciding which path you take. When you are an adult, you realize fully what you missed as a child. And again, you have a choice. You can feel sorry for yourself or you can feel pride at where you came from and where you've gotten to in life. I give thanks to the fact that I grew up poor because it helps me appreciate what I have now."

Taken severally, Sergio's features aren't classically handsome. But they fit together well and his smile further binds them together. Fashion designers love to hang clothes on him. He has a strong physical presence and carries himself with grace. Every now and then, a hard look creeps into his eyes, as though he is remembering the hardships of his youth or the demands of his trade. But he's unfailingly gracious. Women and men are drawn to him.

Boxing was Martinez's route to a better life. "I was a good student," he says. "But my family didn't have the money to continue my education. Without my physical gifts, I don't think I would have found my way out of poverty. But I believe that everyone has a path if they choose to follow it. Everyone has a talent that's special."

Martinez turned pro in 1997 and fought in obscurity for much of his ring career. On June 21, 2003, on what he calls "the most important day of my life," he took a beating but won a twelve-round decision over Richard Williams in Manchester, England, to claim the unheralded IBO 154-pound title.

"It was a very hard fight for me," Sergio recalls, "because I was not experienced at that time. But I won."

One week later, Martinez had a tattoo of a dragon imprinted on the outside of his left arm from shoulder to elbow. In January 2013, he added the word "*resistencia*" (resistance) on the inside of his right forearm and "*victoria*" (victory) on the inside of his left forearm.

"The life I have chosen revolves around those two words," Sergio says, explaining the latter two tattoos. "When I was preparing to fight Chavez [in September 2012], they were constantly in my head. Then I signed to fight Martin Murray. I wasn't motivated, and I thought the tattoos would help motivate me. There will be no more tattoos. I don't like tattoos. I never wanted tattoos. I hate tattoos. It is a contradiction, I know. I cannot explain it except to say, in two brief moments in time, I thought it was important to have these tattoos on my body."

Martinez ascended to stardom on April 17, 2010, when he decisioned Kelly Pavlik to claim the WBC and WBO middleweight crowns. Seven months later, in his first title defense, he scored a dramatic one-punch knockout of Paul Williams. Victories over Sergiy Dzinziruk, Darren Barker, Matthew Macklin, Julio Cesar Chavez, and Martin Murray followed.

"The very poor identify with boxing," Sergio observes. "They look at boxers and relate to the economic conditions that we came from and to our struggle. They admire the courage we have to fight to get to the next level. The very wealthy look at boxers as two animals trying to kill each other for their entertainment. They don't identify on a human level with the fighters. Many of them—I truly believe this—want to see me fail in the end, lose all my money, and go back to nothing. It's like a game for them. And sadly, most boxers who go from very poor to very rich go back quickly to being poor again."

Cotto-Martinez harkened back to a time when New York was the capitol of the sports world. Earlier in the day, California Chrome's pursuit of racing's Triple Crown had drawn a crowd of 102,000 to the Belmont Stakes. On fight night, Madison Square Garden was rocking.

Cotto was bidding to become the first Puerto Rican to win titles in four weight divisions. This would be his ninth fight in the big Garden arena and the first for Martinez. Three thousand fans had attended the Friday weigh-in. It would have been more, but the doors to The Theater at MSG were closed an hour before the fighters stepped on the scales.

Stripped of the hype, Cotto-Martinez was an entertaining match-up between two compelling personalities who have served boxing well. Each man carries himself with dignity. Martinez was a 2-to-1 favorite, but the outcome of the fight was very much in doubt.

The case for a Martinez victory began with the belief that Cotto wasn't "Cotto" anymore. Miguel had lost two fights in a row (to Floyd Mayweather and Austin Trout) before blowing out journeyman Delvin Rodriguez last October. Prior to those fights, he'd been brutalized by

Antonio Margarito and Manny Pacquiao and looked ordinary in victories over Yuri Foreman, Ricardo Mayorga, and (in a rematch) Margarito.

Trout was thought to have given Martinez a roadmap for beating Cotto. Like Sergio, Austin is a tall southpaw. Twelve months earlier, he'd outpointed Miguel 119–109, 117–111, 117–111. Asked at a June 4 sit-down with reporters about the parallels between Trout and Martinez, Cotto responded, "I fought Trout in 2012. Now it is 2014. I never saw that fight after that night, and I have no plans to see it again."

That seemed like a bad case of denial. Moreover, for the first time in a long time, Martinez would be entering the ring with a height (three inches) and weight (four pounds) advantage over his opponent.

"I like to watch my opponents," Martinez says. "I like studying them a lot. More than what they do, it's how they think. I want to know what my opponent is thinking. Once I've seen them, I can figure them out; the ideas they have, their plan, their strategy."

Watching Cotto, Sergio had seen Pacquiao and Mayweather beat Miguel with speed and Margarito beat him with power.

"Cotto does not have the same power at this weight that he had at 147," Martinez opined. "I am the power-puncher of the two of us. When I start to find my rhythm, my timing, and the right distance, the fight will be over."

Team Cotto, of course, held to a contrary view.

Cotto would be the most intelligent and technically skilled opponent that Martinez had faced. Freddie Roach (Miguel's trainer) was confident that edge would enable his fighter to exploit the flaws in Sergio's style.

"Martinez is a great athlete," Roach said. "I wouldn't call him a great boxer. If you keep yourself in a good position, most of the time you'll control the fight. Sergio's footwork is reckless. He's all over the place. Miguel can take advantage of that. And I think Miguel can beat Martinez down the middle. Sergio's defense is not all that good. If you exchange with him, let your hands go, he's very hittable. Chavez didn't do that until the last round, and you saw what happened when he did. I think Cotto's boxing ability will be too much for Martinez to handle."

On the issue of size and power, Cotto declared, "It's not about gaining the weight. It's about not having to lose the weight. For the first time in my career, I'm not concerned about making weight. I can eat to be strong."

"We moved up the weight a little bit and put on more muscle," Roach added. "I think Miguel will be stronger on the inside and much more physical on the inside than Martinez is. We're going to push him around with no problem. On the inside we're the bigger stronger fighter. Sergio is in over his head on this one."

But the biggest issue surrounding Cotto-Martinez was Sergio's physical condition. Some people thought that Cotto was shot. Virtually everyone believed that Martinez was fragile.

Forty-three months had passed since Sergio's demolition of Paul Williams. Subsequent to that, he had looked vulnerable. More than most fighters, Martinez fights with his legs. But in recent fights, his legs have betrayed him.

After decisioning Martin Murray on April 27, 2013, Martinez underwent major knee surgery.

"The recuperation was very painful," Sergio acknowledged in a May 20 teleconference call. "I was on crutches for nine months, and it is very hard to come back from that. But this is the road that I chose, and I enjoy the achievement of coming back from something like this. Right now, I am just the same as when there were no knee problems. I have overcome all obstacles."

That thought was echoed by physical therapist Raquel Bordons, who said in the dressing room an hour before the fight, "Sergio's condition is more than I could have hoped for. He is very very good now."

But at this stage of Martinez's career, injuries during a fight seem as likely as not. Was he fully repaired after the surgery, or was he a thirty-nine-year-old athlete with sub-standard body parts?

Tom Gerbasi framed the issue when he wrote, "It's almost as if Martinez making it to the ring is the equivalent of New York Knicks captain Willis Reed limping out of the tunnel for Game Seven of the NBA Finals against the LA Lakers on May 8, 1970, to inspire his team and get them off to the start they needed to win the game and the title. It's got that feel, that buzz, that for one more night, a great champion can be great. Saturday night is Sergio Martinez's Game Seven. But this is no basketball game. Martinez can't hit two baskets, go back to the bench, and leave his teammates to finish the work like Reed did. This is a fight, twelve rounds with the best fighter Martinez has ever been in with. Thirty-six minutes of wear and tear, physical and mental warfare."

"Who do you like in the fight?" boxing maven Pete Susens was asked.

"Whichever guy has one last big fight left in him," Susens answered.

During the build-up to Cotto-Martinez, Sergio had told the media, "It has been my dream for a long time to fight in the big room at Madison Square Garden."

On fight night, that dream turned into a nightmare.

The heavily pro-Cotto crowd was chanting "Cotto, Cotto" even before the bell to start round one rang. It didn't have to wait long for satisfaction. One minute into the first stanza, Cotto staggered Martinez with a left hook up top. A barrage of punches put Sergio face down on the canvas. He rose on unsteady legs and, a minute later, was decked again by a right hand. Once more, he struggled to his feet. Almost immediately, a body shot put him down for the third time.

That left Martinez with a gaping hole to climb out of on the judges' scorecards. And worse, he was now a debilitated fighter.

"The first punch that hurt me, after that, I never recovered," Sergio said in his dressing room after the fight. "I wasn't the same after that. I couldn't do anything. My mind was disconnected from my body. My mind told me to do something, and my body wouldn't do it."

A brutal beatdown followed. Cotto punished Martinez almost at will to the head and body. Everything that Miguel landed seemed to hurt. Sergio's only hope was that Cotto would fade in the late rounds, as had happened in several recent outings. But with each passing round, it became more unlikely that Martinez would have anything left if and when Cotto faded. As the fight wore on, the question was not who would win, but how much punishment Martinez could take. Sergio wasn't just being outpointed. He was getting beaten up. All that he had left was his heart.

After nine rounds, Pablo Sarmiento stopped the carnage. In the dressing room after the fight, the trainer recounted, "I told him, 'Sergio, champion, you mean more to me than I mean to myself. I am stopping it now.' Sergio pleaded with me, 'One more round.' I told him no, and he accepted that."

If Cotto-Martinez was Miguel's finest hour, it was also Sarmiento's.

As Pablo spoke, Martinez sat on a folding cushioned chair with Raquel Bordons beside him. His face was bruised and swollen. There was a cut on his right eyelid and an ugly gash on top of his head. The right side of his body, where Cotto's left hook had landed again and again, ached. Fortunately, a post-fight trip to Bellevue Hospital for a precautionary MRI revealed nothing more serious than a broken nose.

As for Sergio's future, two things that he has said in the past are instructive.

Prior to fighting Julio Cesar Chavez Jr, Martinez declared, "I always look ahead. That's what works for me; to look toward my goals and never look away from them." Then, in a light moment shortly before fighting Cotto, Sergio acknowledged, "I am thirty-nine, and people think that I'm an old man. For boxing, maybe I am."

Put those thoughts together and retirement after a long and honorable career is a sound option. Meanwhile, Cotto-Martinez stands as a reminder that, for each thrilling victory in boxing, there's a heartbreaking defeat.

The unexpected is part of boxing.

Chris Algieri: An Unlikely Champion

Michael Buffer is unflappable. On fight night, the greatest ring announcer in boxing history is the epitome of cool . . . Composed, collected, imperturbable. Choose your adjective.

Thus, the shock on Buffer's face was telling as he stood in the ring at Barclays Center on June 14, 2014, and reviewed the judges' scorecards one last time before announcing the decision at the end of twelve rounds of action between Ruslan Provodnikov and Chris Algieri.

Provodnikov, a 6-to-1 betting favorite, had scored two first-round knockdowns and been the aggressor throughout the fight. Algieri had spent much of the evening in retreat as a one-eyed fighter. The widespread assumption at ringside was that "The Siberian Rocky" had retained his 140-pound WBO title by a comfortable margin.

It was the end of a long night.

Earlier in the evening, local favorite Heather Hardy was awarded a horrible decision over Jackie Trivilino in a fight that went to the scorecards after seven rounds due to a severe cut suffered by Hardy as a consequence of an accidental head butt. Fight fans want their fighter to win. But they also have a sense of fairness. There were a lot of boos when Hardy's victory was announced by a 68–65, 67–66, 66–67 margin.

Then, in round three of a junior-welterweight bout, Fedor Papazov decked Miguel Angel Mendoza with a picture-perfect right hand. Mendoza rose on wobbly legs. Everything else about him was wobbling too. It's unclear what referee Gary Rosato was watching at the time. But it didn't appear to be Mendoza, because Rosato motioned for the action to continue. Fortunately, ring doctor Avery Browne climbed onto the ring apron and stopped the fight.

After that, unbeaten light-heavyweight Seanie Monaghan continued his maturation by pounding out a lopsided ten-round decision over thirty-five-year-old Elvir Muriqi. Muriqi is now a respectable 40 and 7 with

24 knockouts and only 1 KO by. But over the course of sixteen years, his career has gone from prospect to journeyman without much in between.

Next up was Demetrius Andrade vs. Brian Rose, another of boxing's unfortunate "mandatory" title defenses (in this instance, for the WBO 154-pound belt).

Andrade-Rose was a woeful mismatch from beginning to end. There wasn't one moment when the outcome of the fight was in doubt. Demetrius circled his opponent throughout the bout, knocking him down in the first and third rounds and pounding on him like he was a heavy bag. Rose wasn't good enough to make things boring (let alone, interesting). It was just plain ugly. The challenger's corner correctly stopped the carnage at 1:19 of round seven when the usually reliable referee Mike Griffin failed to do so.

That set the stage for Provodnikov-Algieri.

Fans want to see exciting fights. Provodnikov, age thirty, is an exciting fighter. He attacks with ferocity, hits and gets hit, and engages in wars of attrition.

"To be honest, I am not one of the most talented boxers," Ruslan acknowledged at a June 7 media sitdown. "But I fight my hardest for every minute of every round."

Provodnikov's non-stop aggression and brawling swarming style had led him to a 23-and-2 record with 16 knockouts. The losses were by decision to Tim Bradley and Mauricio Herrera. His most recent victory was a tenth-round stoppage of Mike Alvarado that brought him the WBO belt.

"The championship and the belt are not as important to me as the respect of the fans," Ruslan told the media.

"Provodnikov," Tom Gerbasi wrote, "is what we hope a prizefighter will be. He gives his all in the ring, entertains. And when it's over, he's the kind of guy you wouldn't mind shooting the breeze with over a plate of raw moose liver."

Algieri is as different from Provodnikov as Huntington, Long Island, is different from Siberia.

Boxing fans can count on one finger the number of fighters who have an undergraduate degree from Stony Brook College and a master's in nutrition from New York Institute of Technology. Algieri is the one.

"I don't fight because I have to," Chris says. "I fight because I want to fight."

Algieri looks younger than his thirty years and has a nice way about him. He's articulate and smart and, in addition to pursuing his boxing career, works as a nutritionist.

"The best thing about being a fighter," Algieri notes, "is the incentive I get to stay fit, work out, focus on what I eat, and stay healthy. I eat the same whether I'm in training for a fight or not."

In six years as a pro, Chris had posted a 19-and-0 record. But the opposition had been undistinguished and he'd scored only eight knockouts.

"I can beat Provodnikov," Algieri said at the same media sitdown. "Boxing is a rhythm sport. If I can keep him from establishing his rhythm, I win the fight. I plan to box, use my legs and jab. I'm an endurance guy. I get stronger as a fight goes on. Everyone I've fought had a game plan to get inside, punch, push me around, break me down. No one has been able to do it yet."

"Home-run hitters strike out more than regular guys," Chris added.

But in boxing, it only takes one home run to win the game.

When fight night came, Provodnikov-Algieri appeared to be over in the first round.

Provodnikov came out aggressively, and Algieri simply couldn't keep him off. Just past the midway point of the first stanza, a left hook up top put Chris on the canvas for the first time in his career and raised an ugly swelling around his right eye. Later in the round, Algieri took a knee (scored as a second knockdown) to collect himself.

Thereafter, Algieri fought as well as he could; moving, jabbing, and landing sharp crisp punches. Often, he used his speed and four-inch height advantage to outbox Provodnikov. But Chris's blows lacked power, and Ruslan kept coming forward. It seemed to be just a matter of time before body shots took Algieri's legs away from him and he'd be unable to move out of harm's way.

By the late rounds, the right side of Algieri's face was black and blue, purple, and a few other colors, in addition to being grotesquely swollen. His eye was shut and it looked as though an alien creature was trapped inside the mess, struggling to get out. But Chris kept moving and throwing punches. He didn't crumble physically or mentally in the face of Provodnikov's pressure assault. Like Ruslan, he fought the fight he wanted to fight.

Pride, guts, courage; Algieri showed them all.

Then came the decision of the judges: Max DeLuca 117–109 in favor of Provodnikov . . . Tom Schreck and Don Trella 114–112 in favor of Algieri.

Since then, the decision has been widely criticized. I was among the early critics. On fight night, I scored the bout 116–111 (7-4-1 in rounds) for Provodnikov.

After the fact, I learned that CompuBox recorded Algieri outlanding Provodnikov by a 288-to-205 margin. That didn't sway me. Further to that point, according to CompuBox, Algieri outlanded Provodnikov in every round but the twelfth (when Ruslan had a 13-to-11 margin). But "punches landed" aren't dispositive of scoring issues. This is professional boxing, not amateur competition. Like knockdowns, hard punches should be weighted more heavily than pitty-pats.

For example, in round one, Algieri had an 18-to-14 edge in punches landed. And everyone in the arena scored that round 10–7 in favor of Provodnikov.

One of the first people I discussed Provodnikov-Algieri with afterward was Paulie Malignaggi (who'd been at ringside covering the bout for British television). Paulie scored it for Algieri. That wasn't entirely unpredictable. In some respects, the fight had resembled the June 10, 2006, confrontation between Malignaggi and Miguel Cotto.

"Provodnikov won the first round big," Paulie told me. "But after the first round, you can't score the damage on Chris's face. You give Provodnikov credit for busting Chris up and knocking him down twice in the first round, but that's it. After that, you score it round by round, each round individually, as though Chris's face was clean."

Eighteen hours later, I watched a replay of Provodnikov-Algieri on television. This was one of those rare occasions when watching a fight a day later caused me to adjust my scorecard. Viewing the replay, it seemed to me that Provodnikov was less effective after round one than I'd originally thought. I still think Ruslan won the fight. But it was close.

Meanwhile, Algieri came to the post-fight press conferences wearing dark glasses and holding an icepack to his forehead.

"I could see pretty well until the eighth round," Chris told the media. "By the time we hit round twelve, I was blind in that eye. But I was able to anticipate his left hook throughout the fight. I was able to figure out his rhythm. That was the key to my success. The big thing was getting out of the first round."

Algieri had fought so valiantly and through such adversity that even those who thought Provodnikov had won found it hard to begrudge Chris his triumph.

Vitali Klitschko has said, "It's very important in life to have a dream." Boyd Melson has a dream.

Boyd Melson: An Atypical Fighter

People tend to stereotype fighters. Boyd Melson is not your average fighter. Then again, he's not your average West Point graduate or your average Jewish kid from Westchester or your average anything.

Melson's maternal grandparents were born in Poland and were Holocaust survivors. His grandfather escaped from a train that was en route to an extermination camp and joined the Russian Army in the war against Nazi Germany. His father, who spent twenty-six years in the United States military, is Louisiana Creole with African American, French, Spanish, and Cherokee roots. Boyd's sister is an officer in the US Army Judge Advocate Group. His brother is in a public-health doctoral program at New York Medical College.

Melson is thoughtful, affable, and a talker.

"I was raised as a black male, and I'm Jewish," Boyd says. "But I'm open to different religions." Then he elaborates, saying, "Religions are the same in a lot of ways. They're just written differently. I believe that the highest power in the world is love. I believe that God exists in every one of us, but it's not Him or Her or It that's making things happen. It helps us to think that someone else is responsible for what goes on because it takes the burden off of us. But we're all responsible for what we do and who we are. Bad things can happen for no good reason or because someone planned them to happen. You can ask, 'Why do people get cancer?' But you can also ask, 'Why do people do bad things to each other?' Good things are the same way. Some good things happen by accident, and some good things happen by design. Loving human beings is my identity. I take that very seriously. Everything else in my life complements that."

Those thoughts might sound incongruous coming from a professional fighter, particularly one who graduated from the United States Military Academy at West Point. After all, the sweet science and the United States Army aren't the first things that come to mind when the average person thinks of "love." But they're part of the mosaic that's Melson's life.

West Point was a transformative experience for him.

"I'd heard stories about plebe year at West Point and thought getting yelled at would be funny." Melson recalls. "That lasted about ten minutes. Then shock set in. I can't really explain what the experience was like. But in the end, West Point teaches you to believe in yourself. You learn to sift through the crap to get to your objective. You learn that, no matter how bad something is, it will pass. You develop confidence that, no matter bad things are, you'll find a way to get to where you want to be. You learn how to handle stress with everything—I mean everything—on the line."

As part of the West Point curriculum, all plebes (first-year cadets) are required to take a boxing class that consists of twenty forty-five-minute lessons. The last four classes are graded bouts. Each plebe engages in four bouts with two one-minute rounds in each contest.

The purpose of the class isn't to teach boxing skills as much as it's to instill mental toughness; to teach young men to face their fears and prepare for that moment down the road in military combat when they have only themselves to rely on.

"When you're in combat," Melson explains, "it's not about American freedom at that particular moment in time. It's about you and your buddies surviving. In boxing, you're trying to hurt someone to win, and that person is trying to hurt you. You learn to think and make decisions under stress. You train your mind to not give up before your body does. Military combat is far more serious than boxing, but some of the demands are the same."

Melson won all four of his plebe bouts and went from there into intramural boxing. Then he joined the intercollegiate boxing team.

"Eventually," he recalls, "word began filtering through the ranks that this crazy plebe was knocking people out."

Melson graduated from West Point in 2003. His first assignment after matriculation was to teach plebe boxing at West Point. Then, after four-and-a-half months of artillery school, he was assigned to the US Army World Class Athlete Program, which trains Army personnel to compete at the national and international level with the ultimate goal of making the United States Olympic Team. He won numerous amateur honors and was a four-time United States Army champion.

Melson stopped boxing in November 2007 after failing to qualify for the United States Olympic Team. On May 31, 2008, he completed his five-year military commitment and took a job in corporate America, selling spinal implants for Medtronic (a leader in the development and manufacture of medical devices).

The new career fit nicely with a passion that Boyd had developed. On June 22, 2002, toward the end of his junior year at West Point, he'd met a woman named Christan Zaccagnino at a dance club. Christan had been wheelchair-bound since age ten after breaking her neck in a diving accident.

A relationship followed. And while Boyd and Christan haven't been romantically involved since 2009, he still describes her as his "soulmate."

Melson's relationship with Christan led him to become a forceful advocate for stem-cell research.

"I've spent the past twelve years of my life trying to help Christan walk again," Boyd says. "And that effort has turned into a quest to get all people who've suffered spinal cord injuries out of their chairs. I've spent a lot of time educating myself on paralysis and neurology and neuroscience and stem cells so I can understand the issues."

"The hypocrisy and ignorance that surrounds the political debate over stem-cell research is incredibly frustrating to me," Melson continues. "People are so ignorant on the issue. To give you one example; stem cells don't just come from abortions. Stem cells can come from umbilical cords after a baby is born. One reason I wanted to make the US Olympic Team was I'd heard that, if you won a gold medal, you'd get to shake hands with the president of the United States. I had a vision of winning a gold medal, meeting George Bush at the White House, and shaking hands with him so hard that it crushed the nerves in his hand and he needed stem-cell treatment to get the function back in his hand. Would I really have done it? Probably not. But I would have wanted to. And I have a very strong grip."

Melson left Medtronic after two years and took a job as a medical-device sales representative for Johnson & Johnson. "But over time," he says, "a sadness came over me. I couldn't figure it out. Then I realized it was because I was no longer trying to do something amazing and different from anyone else. I wanted to do something special. That meant I wanted to box again."

Boyd resumed training in summer 2010, and turned pro with a four-round triumph over Andrew Jones on November 20 of that year. His professional record to date is 14 wins against 1 loss and a draw with 4 knockouts. The loss came by decision in an eight-round war against Delen Parsley. Melson was on the canvas once and Parsley twice.

Melson's primary income now comes from teaching boxing and physical conditioning classes at Equinox (a national health club) and training a handful of private clients. He donates his fight purses to justadollarplease. org, a non-profit organization that raises funds for research at The Spinal Cord Injury Project at the W. M. Keck Center for Collaborative Neuroscience (affiliated with Rutgers University). In addition, Boyd and Christan have co-founded Team Fight to Walk, a 501(c)(3) corporation that raises money for Just a Dollar Please and will continue to support other research ventures after the clinical trials at Rutgers are complete.

"When Christopher Reeve died, we lost our celebrity," Melson says. "I'm fighting to get attention, but not for myself. It's for the cause."

What sort of a future does Melson have in boxing?

He's a thirty-two-year-old southpaw without much power who gets hit too much.

"I don't see him cracking the top ten in any legitimate rankings," Showtime boxing analyst Steve Farhood says. "But he's a great guy. And for his own sense of competitiveness, I hope he gets the chance to test himself at least once in the bigtime."

Ron Katz (one of the savviest matchmakers in the business) is in accord and adds, "Very few people are blessed with the physical gifts you need to be a great fighter. Boyd doesn't have those gifts. But he enjoys boxing. He does the best he can with what he has and gives it his all. There are far more talented fighters out there who don't bring honor to the sport the way Boyd does."

"I'm boxing because there's so much that I love about it," Melson says. "I love the physical and the intellectual competition, the me versus you. It's competition in its most basic form. You have to be willing to suffer in training to get to where you want to be. You have to be a masochist to do what you have to do. You have to be cruel to yourself to be a fighter. If you're not pushing yourself to misery, you're not preparing yourself properly."

"For me, there's always that moment in the dressing room before a fight when they bring the gloves in. I say to myself, 'I must be crazy; I'm never doing this again.' But at the same time, I want to get in the ring so I can make happen what I want to happen. Then I get in the ring. My adrenalin is flowing. I know I'm going to get hurt; it's just a question of how much. I get hit in the face. And unless it's on the nose or in the eye, it feels like pressure, that's all. Getting hit on the back of the head hurts. Getting hit in the throat, sometimes I can't breathe. All body shots hurt."

And what goes through Melson's mind when he hits someone?

"I hope I hurt him. In the military, very often, you're trying to kill people. In boxing—let's be honest about this—you're trying to hurt people. Before the world was civilized, we were here to survive and procreate. Boxing brings you back to that. To survive, you conquer. But in both disciplines—military combat and boxing—you rely on brotherhood and you're surrounded by love. You can only tap in to a certain level with anger, and then it runs dry. You can tap in deeper with love."

Would Melson be boxing if he'd been deployed in the military and seen combat?

"I don't know," he answers. "I might have come back angry and had an even greater need to fight. Or I might have come back and said 'that's enough.'"

Melson is now slated to fight Glen Tapia on the undercard of Gennady Golovkin vs. Daniel Geale at Madison Square Garden on July 26. A lot of people who care about Boyd don't like the fight.

Tapia is twenty-four years old with a 21-and 1 record and 13 knockouts. His one loss was a brutal beatdown at the hands of James Kirkland in Atlantic City last December. But before being stopped, Tapia had Kirkland in trouble.

Boyd is on the card because he sells tickets. For the first time in his pro career, he'll be a heavy underdog.

"I know I'm the opponent going in," Melson says. "But it's a dream of mine to fight at Madison Square Garden. I've fought at Barclays Center twice and Boardwalk Hall in Atlantic City twice. Those are great places but they're not the Garden. I don't know how far I'll go in boxing, but this is an opportunity for me to get to the next level. I want to be on the card, and I'm willing to be the B-side fighter. It's an opportunity for me to test myself and build on what I accomplished in my last fight."

That fight took place on February 12, 2014, at Roseland Ballroom in New York against a club fighter named Donald Ward. It was supposed to be an easy victory for Melson. But in round three, he injured his brachial plexus (a network of nerve fibers running from the spine through his neck into his right arm).

"The pain was excruciating," Boyd recalls. "I couldn't control my arm. I couldn't feel my fingers in my glove. I thought I was having a stroke. My first thought was, 'I don't know what's happening to my body. I'm scared. I have to quit.' I started to turn to take a knee. Then I thought about my training at West Point. To survive in combat and in the ring, you slow time down around you when, in reality, real time is taking place. You gut it out and do whatever you have to do to survive. That's what I try to do for every second of every fight. That's what I did that night."

From that point on, Melson was a wounded soldier. "I was barely able to move my right arm," he recalls. "I landed only one good right hand all night after that—a right hook—and it almost threw me into shock."

But he survived and won a majority decision.

"Of all my fights, that's the one that's the most meaningful to me," Boyd says. "It confirmed what I've always believed about myself; that I can overcome the worst kind of adversity and do what I have to do to prevail. The idea of quitting kept trying to creep into my head. But I was able to block out worrying about my injury and stay in the moment when I couldn't move my arm and didn't know what had happened to me and suppress the fear and do what I had to do to win. It's not just about how far I can go in boxing. It's about testing myself and enjoying the journey."

"I love boxing," Melson says, summing up. "It's the ultimate experience for testing physical ability and intelligence under threat of the greatest adverse consequences possible short of death. And I love being called upon to comport myself with dignity when I'm in the spotlight, competing in a sport that some people think is barbaric but I think is wonderful."

Boxing fans won't know how good Gennady Golovkin is until he finds elite inquisitors who are willing to test him.

GGG = WOW

On July 26, 2014, at Madison Square Garden, Gennady Golovkin took another step on what he hopes will be a march toward greatness when he knocked out Daniel Geale in the third round.

The thirty-two-year-old Golovkin, a native of Kazakhstan, has risen dramatically in the public consciousness since knocking out Gregorz Proksa in a September 1, 2012, bout on HBO. There were 685,000 "real time" viewers for that fight. In three succeeding fights, real time viewership rose to 813,000 (for Golovkin vs. Gabriel Rosado), 1.1 million (vs. Matthew Macklin), and 1.4 million (vs. Curtis Stevens).

Prior to entering the ring against Geale, Golovkin's ring ledger showed 29 wins in 29 fights with 26 knockouts. The last time an opponent went the distance with him was six years and eighteen fights ago. He's the most impressive of the WBA's many middleweight champions.

Geale, a thirty-three-year-old Australian and former IBF beltholder, came into the fight with a 30-and-2 record, including 16 knockouts. The two losses were by split decision against Darren Barker and Anthony Mundine. Geale had never been knocked out, but he'd never beaten an elite fighter either. In fact, he'd never fought one.

Golovkin's life has been shadowed by tragedy. Two of his brothers were killed in military combat (in 1990 and 1994). More recently, on February 18 of this year, his father died of a sudden heart attack. The pain of that experience was very much on Gennady's face when he answered questions about his father's death at a June 7 kick-off press conference for Golovkin-Geale in New York.

"This is life," Gennady said. "I understand. It is hard, but I must go on."

Golovkin was a 10-to-1 favorite to beat Geale. They had met in the ring as amateurs at the 2001 East Asian Games with Gennady winning a clear-cut decision. But what they'd done as pros was far more relevant.

Geale is a competent fighter. Golovkin looks like a great one.

Abel Sanchez (Golovkin's trainer) put matters in perspective when he observed, "Prior to the fights, Gennady's opponents are respectful but they're not scared. Then the fight starts, they get hit, and things change. They stop thinking about winning and start thinking about surviving. Gennady hurts his opponents. Geale is used to going twelve rounds, but he's not used to going twelve rounds against Gennady."

"This is boxing," Golovkin cautioned. "I am not super-hero. I am good fighter, but the opponent doesn't just lie down. You have to work to knock him out, and that cannot always happen."

That said, it was taken for granted by most people in boxing that Golovkin would beat Geale. The issue was, "How decisively and how dramatically would it happen?"

Golovkin-Geale marked the second fight card in seven weeks in the main arena at Madison Square Garden. The attendance was announced as 8,572. But there were ticket discounts and some freebies thrown in to get to that number.

The first three fights of the evening were pathetic mismatches.

Julian Rodriguez knocked out Yankton Southern in forty-three seconds. To put that achievement in perspective, Southern was also knocked out in one round by Chris Hill (who has four wins in thirty-two fights).

Next, Dusty Hernandez-Harrison ran his record to 23 and 0 by decisioning Wilfredo Acuna (80–72 times three on the judges' scorecards). Acuna has lost 8 of his last 9 fights (with the win coming against an opponent who has an 0-and-7 record and been knocked out seven times).

Then cruiserweight Ola Afolabi (199 pounds) battered Anthony Caputo Smith, who was knocked out ten months go by Seanie Monaghan at 175 pounds. The bloody slaughter was stopped by the ring doctor after the third round (twenty-one seconds longer than it took Monaghan to do the job last year).

That was followed by Bryant Jennings vs. Mike Perez.

At the final pre-fight press conference on July 23, Jennings told the media, "Come Saturday night, you're definitely going to see the two best heavyweights in the world."

Today's heavyweights are bad, but not that bad.

Jennings is a limited fighter, but at least he looks the part. Perez came into the ring looking like he'd spent the early part of the month competing in the Nathan's Fourth of July Hot Dog Eating Contest and, after eating 110 hot dogs in thirty minutes, celebrating by drinking a gallon of beer.

It was a sloppy inartful fight that lasted for twelve stultifying rounds. Perez tired noticeably from the fourth round on. Late in the final stanza, referee Harvey Dock deducted a point from him for intentionally hitting on the break. The deduction was appropriate given the fact that the foul was blatant and Perez had fought a chippy fight throughout the evening. In the end, that point was determinative of the outcome. Jennings won a split decision by a 115–112, 114–113, 113–114 margin.

Then it was time for Golovkin-Geale.

"Golovkin's opponents," Hamilton Nolan has written, "are generally regarded in the same way that visitors to a pet store regard the mice being lowered into a snake's cage at feeding time."

There's an inexorable quality to the way Gennady fights. He's a pressure fighter, who cuts off the ring well and manages to control the distance between himself and his opponent. Every move is purposeful.

Geale tried to fight aggressively and get off first, but it was to no avail. Twenty seconds into round two, an accumulation of punches punctuated by a glancing right hand high on the head deposited him on the canvas. By the end of the round, his face and body language had the look of a beaten fighter.

In round three, the loss became official. With thirty seconds left in the stanza, Geale landed a straight right hand. Golovkin took it and returned fire instantaneously with a straight right of his own that landed smack in the center of Daniel's face and put him flat on his back. Geale rose, but his head was spinning and he had a bad case of the wobbles. With Daniel's wholehearted concurrence, referee Mike Ortega stopped the fight.

Given the idiocy of the world sanctioning bodies, the term "champion" has been sadly devalued in recent years. Golovkin is now the WBA "super world middleweight champion." As of this writing, the WBA also has the following similarly-titled "world champions":

WBA super world super-middleweight champion = Andre Ward

WBA unified world super-middleweight champion = Carl
Froch

WBA interim world super-middleweight champion =
Stanyslav Kashtanov

WBA interim world middleweight champion = Dmitriy
Chudinov

In addition, the WBA "world middleweight championship" will be
contested between Jarrod Fletcher and Danny Jacobs on August 9.

So forget lineal, super-duper, and all the other ridiculous belts. Miguel
Cotto might have a claim on some mythical championship by virtue of
his recent victory over Sergio Martinez. But ask ten experts who would
win a fight between Golovkin and Cotto, and the likelihood is that all
ten would pick Gennady. At present, Golovkin is the true middleweight
champion. Any middleweight who takes issue with that proposition
should fight him.

Gennady is a relatively small middleweight. He comes into training
camp at just under 170 pounds. Making weight is easy for him. If the
money is right, he'll fight anyone from 154 to 168 pounds. That would
put Floyd Mayweather, Canelo Alvarez, and Cotto at the top of his wish
list. But it's unlikely that any of those three will go near him.

Andre Ward, Carl Froch, and Julio Cesar Chavez Jr are the big names
at 168 pounds. But Froch has already said "no" to a Golovkin fight, and
neither Ward nor Chavez seems anxious for the test. Look for the other
middleweight beltholders (like Peter Quillin) to also avoid him.

Golovkin isn't unbeatable. Every fighter is limited in one way or
another. But it will take a great fighter to beat Gennady at the level
he's fighting at now. And as long as the other top fighters from 154 to
168 pounds avoid him, they should rate behind him. Indeed, one can
argue that, right now, Golovkin is the #1 pound-for-pound fighter in
the world.

If Floyd Mayweather disputes that notion, let him fight Gennady at
154 pounds.

Trust me; Floyd won't.

In 2014, the fights kept coming in New York.

New York Notes

Boxing fans know all about the rivalry between Top Rank and Golden Boy. Also, HBO versus Showtime. But in New York, there's another nascent competition: Madison Square Garden versus Barclays Center.

For decades, Madison Square Garden was "the Mecca of boxing." That time is long gone. But until recently, The Garden was the premier destination for big fights in The Big Apple. Last year, Barclays challenged that notion.

There were three fight cards at Madison Square Garden in 2013; all of them in the smaller venue known as The Theater, not the main arena. The headline attractions on those cards were: January 19—Gennady Golovkin vs. Gabriel Rosado, Orlando Salido vs. Mikey Garcia, Roman Martinez vs. Juan Carlos Burgos . . . April 20—Tyson Fury vs. Steve Cunningham, Curtis Stevens vs. Derrick Findley . . . November 2— Gennady Golovkin vs. Curtis Stevens, Magomed Abdusalamov vs. Mike Perez.

By contrast, there were five fight cards at Barclays Center in 2013: March 9—Bernard Hopkins vs. Tavoris Cloud, Keith Thurman vs. Jan Zaveck . . . April 27—Danny Garcia vs. Zab Judah, Peter Quillin vs. Fernando Guerrero . . . June 22—Paulie Malignaggi vs. Adrien Broner, Seth Mitchell vs. Johnathon Banks . . . September 30—Michael Perez vs. Miguel Zuniga, Sadam Ali vs. Jay Krupp . . . December 7—Paulie Malignaggi vs. Zab Judah, Devon Alexander vs. Shawn Porter, Erislandy Lara vs. Austin Trout, Sakio Bika vs. Anthony Dirrell.

Golovkin is the best fighter in that group. But Barclays had a credible claim to the more impressive line-up.

2014 began with fight cards at both sites within the span of five days. First, on January 25, HBO telecast a doubleheader from Madison Square Garden featuring Mikey Garcia vs. Juan Carlos Burgos and Bryant Jennings vs. Artur Szpilka. The opening undercard bout was scheduled for 6:30 pm. The first HBO fight began at ten o'clock. That left three-and-a-half hours for six undercard fights, four of which ended in the first round and one in the second. There was a lot of down time.

Ten years ago, Jennings-Szpilka would have been a mid-level offering on Cedric Kushner's *Heavyweight Explosion* series. Jennings is vying for a rung on the world-class heavyweight ladder. Szpilka is a club fighter. But the excitement generated by Artur's fans gave the contest drama. Bryant tried throughout the bout to load up on a big right hand. Then, late in the going, he realized that the left hook was there for the landing.

Szpilka has a questionable chin. In round ten, a hook to the jaw deposited Artur on the lowest of the four ring strands. He rose, woozy and unable to defend himself. Referee Mike Ortega, showing poor judgment, instructed the fighters to resume fighting. Then, perhaps remembering what happened to Magomed Abdusalamov in the same ring on November 2 of last year, Dr. Barry Jordan (medical director for the New York State Athletic Commission), climbed onto the ring apron and stopped the bout. Whether Jennings is America's next world-class heavyweight or the next Seth Mitchell remains to be seen.

Many of Szpilka's fans left immediately after the bout, and the energy in the arena rapidly dissipated. The atmosphere for Garcia-Burgos was sepulcher in nature. Nor did the fight help. Garcia is a patient technically sound fighter who gets the job done. Burgos is a capable boxer, who didn't have the firepower to hurt Garcia and seemed happy to survive for twelve rounds, collect his money, and go home. The bout had the feel of a sparring session, with Garcia winning by scores of 119–109, 118–110, 118–110.

Five nights later, on January 30, the scene moved southeast to Barclays Center, a fifteen-minute ride on the subway from Manhattan to Brooklyn. Fox Sports 1 was the host network. The non-televised undercard featured 5-and-0 vs. 3-and-6, 13-and-0 vs. 7-and-7, and 8-and-0 vs. 4-and-8.

The worst match-up of the evening was 23-and-0 Gary Russell Jr vs. Miguel Tamayo of Mexico. Russell is being maneuvered to a title bout without being legitimately tested. Tomayo had lost three of his previous four fights with the only win in that span coming against a sub-.500 plodder. Russell-Tomayo might have been designed to make boxing fans eager to see more of Russell. It certainly made them want to see less of Tomayo. A predictable knockout followed.

Then Eddie Gomez (another prospect being carefully groomed) pounded out a workmanlike unanimous decision over Danquan Arnett. Future opponents might take note of the fact that Gomez tends to drop his right hand when he throws his hook up top.

That set the table for the main event: Victor Ortiz vs. Luis Collazo.

Ortiz entered the ring one day short of his twenty-seventh birthday with a 29-4-2 record and widespread doubt regarding his mental fortitude. He'd won only once in the preceding forty months (an April 16, 2011, decision over Andre Berto) and was coming off back-to-back knockout losses at the hands of Floyd Mayweather (sucker-punch) and Josesito Lopez (broken jaw).

Collazo, thirty-two years old, sported a 34-and-5 record. He's a faded version of the fighter who lost a razor-thin decision to Ricky Hatton seven years ago and tested Andre Berto three years after that.

Ortiz fought aggressively in round one, but lacked the hard edge he'd shown when his career was on-track. Late in round two, the fighters (both southpaws) threw right hooks simultaneously. Collazo's landed. Victor stumbled backward. Luis followed with two glancing blows, and Ortiz went down. Whether Victor could have gotten up is a matter of conjecture. What's clear is that he didn't, nor did he seem to try. He was counted out at 2:59 of the stanza.

Ortiz's vulnerability, both in and out of the ring, makes him a compelling figure. That said; this was the most troubling of his losses. Collazo is not a big puncher and had scored only four knockouts in the previous eight years.

More significantly, Ortiz wasn't taking a beating (as he had in his loss against Marcos Maidana). His jaw wasn't dangerously broken (as it was against Josesito Lopez). If he'd beaten the count, he would have had a full minute to recover. Fighters come back from knockdowns like that to win fights. Indeed, Victor did it against Andre Berto. But that Victor Ortiz exists now only in memory.

Whatever Ortiz once had as a fighter, he doesn't have it anymore. The good part of his career is over. Let's hope that the rest of the end game is short.

★ ★ ★

After a while, the big arenas where fights are held start to feel the same. The spectator areas, dressing rooms, and ringside corrals have a homogenous look. Small venues are more likely to have their own unique character.

Roseland had character. It opened as a ballroom in 1919 at Broadway and 51st Street in New York. Thirty-seven years later, the building was torn down and ballroom dancers were redirected to what had once been a skating rink one block to the north.

In the decades that followed, Roseland hosted everything from gala parties to rock concerts. Guests sang "Happy Birthday" to Hillary Clinton and listened enthralled as the Rolling Stones blasted out "Satisfaction."

Time marches on. Roseland will close its doors after an April 7, 2014, concert by Lady Gaga. Then it will be demolished to make way for a high-rise building.

Roseland was never identified with boxing in the public mind. But over the years, twenty-seven fight cards were contested there. An over-hanging balcony offered spectators a spectacular view of the ring. There wasn't a bad seat in the house.

The first boxing event held at Roseland was a Cedric Kushner *Heavyweight Explosion* card on December 8, 1998, featuring Al Cole vs. Kirk Johnson, Obed Sullivan vs. Jesse Ferguson, and Shannon Briggs vs. Marcus Rhode. Three months later, Kushner returned with Hasim Rahman vs. Michael Rush and Danell Nicholson vs. Frankie Swindell. Rahman KO'd Rush in five rounds. Two years later, he knocked out Lennox Lewis in South Africa to become heavyweight champion of the world.

Paulie Malignaggi won his second pro fight at Roseland with a fourth-round stoppage of Robert Sowers on July 26, 2001. He was there again on November 23 of that year to fight on a card promoted by Lou DiBella with the proceeds going to the families of police officers and firefighters who had died on 9/11. Future champions Jermain Taylor and Orlando Salido also emerged victorious that night. But the show ended on a horrifying note when James Butler (who lost a unanimous decision to Richard Grant in the main event) sucker-punched Grant as the victor stood in the ring awaiting a post-fight television interview.

It was a horrifying moment. Grant dropped to the canvas. Blood poured from his mouth. His jaw was fractured and he went into convulsions. Butler was arrested on the spot. He later pled guilty to felony assault, served four months in prison, and was released on five year's probation. He is now in prison again subsequent to a guilty plea in conjunction with the 2004 murder of writer Sam Kellerman.

Five years passed after the Butler-Grant fiasco before boxing returned to Roseland. The most glorious moment in the ballroom's ring history occurred on July 15, 2011, when Pawel Wolak and Delvin Rodriguez fought to a ten-round draw that evoked memories of the first encounter between Arturo Gatti and Micky Ward.

David Tua, Peter Quillin, Yuri Foreman, David Telesco, and Louis Del Valle also fought at Roseland. The final bell tolled on Wednesday night (February 12, 2014), when DiBella Entertainment promoted the last fight card that the one-time ballroom will ever host.

Wednesday's fights started shortly after 7:00 pm The seats filled up early. Soon only standing room was available. Curtis Jackson III (better known as 50 Cent) was there. So was Rosie Perez. Stephen Espinoza and Gordon Hall were onhand to scout future opponents for ShoBox. Harold Lederman and Peter Nelson gave HBO a presence.

There were nine fights, most of them well matched with spirited action. If one imagined that the fighters' gloves were black, their trunks black or white, and the ring canvas tan, it could have been the 1940s.

Ron Rizzo (vice president of operations for DiBella Entertainment) stood in the balcony, overlooking the scene. "For me, the closing is personal," Rizzo said. "I was working for Cedric when we did the first show here. Roseland always had a special feel to it. There's enough room and enough open space that you can move around and socialize between fights. Wherever you are, you get a good look at the ring. In all the years I've been in boxing, I haven't found a place I like as much as this. I'll miss it."

Those thoughts resonated with Kushner, who was sitting quietly on a banquette toward the rear of the arena. These are hard times for Cedric. Once, he was at the center of the boxing universe. In recent years, he has suffered reversals.

How did Kushner feel about Roseland closing?

"It's a sign of the times," Cedric said. "And for me, personally, it's another part of my past, gone."

★ ★ ★

If one wanted to construct an argument for the abolition of professional boxing, the August 9, 2014, fight card at Barclays Center in Brooklyn would be a good place to start. The undercard featured three first-round knockouts (one at the twenty-eight-second mark) and some horrible judging in favor of house fighter Zachary Ochoa. But in some respects, the three featured fights were worse.

Danny Garcia, who might be the best 140-pound fighter in the world, brutally knocked out pathetically overmatched, 50-to-1 underdog Rod Salka in the second round.

Lamont Peterson (who was pummeled into submission by Lucas Matthysse last year) played it safe by going in against shopworn thirty-five-year-old Edgar Santana, a 33-to-1 underdog. Peterson loaded up and threw punches at Santana (who looked like he was auditioning for the role of a heavy bag) all night. It was a horrible ugly one-sided beating that ended when New York State Athletic Commission medical director Barry Jordan intervened in round ten (which was five rounds too late). Santana will pay for the punishment he took for the rest of his life.

But as bad as Garcia-Salka and Peterson-Santana were, the fight that did the most to tarnish boxing might have been Danny Jacobs vs. Jarrod Fletcher.

For more than a century, the term "world champion" had special meaning and was part of a long and glorious tradition.

No more.

The single most-damaging development in boxing in recent years has been the proliferation of world "champions." There are now as many as one hundred of them at any given time. Fans simply don't know who the champions are.

Jacobs-Fletcher was for a bogus "world championship." Fletcher didn't even perform like a good club fighter. Jacobs, who four years ago was knocked out by the only world-class fighter he ever faced, ended matters in round five.

I like Danny Jacobs. He's a nice young man. His comeback from cancer is an inspiring story. I wish him every success. Outside the ring, he carries himself like a champion. Maybe someday he'll be a champion inside the ring too. But right now, he isn't.

★ ★ ★

On October 15, 2014, Heather Hardy (10-0 with 2 knockouts) fought Crystal Hoy at B. B. King's in New York for what the WBC calls its "international female super-bantamweight championship." Hoy came into the bout on a five-fight winless streak and had won two of her last eleven outings dating back to 2005.

When asked what qualified Hoy to fight for a WBC championship, WBC president Mauricio Sulaiman told this writer, "Whatever I respond, you will write what you imagine and whatever you want to relay to your readers. I am personally very confident of this match. It will be a good competitive fight."

WBC supervisor Jill Diamond was more expansive in her response, noting in part, "Records don't tell the total story. Crystal has an extensive bio and has fought some very tough women, a few who went on to be world champions. She's missed out on some close decisions and stood her ground. And her last fight, also to a good fighter, was a draw, not a loss."

The "good fighter" referenced by Ms. Diamond has one win in her last six fights.

Further to Ms. Diamond's point, according to BoxRec.com, six of the women who beat Hoy have been "champions" at one time or another.

Nydia Feliciano won the vacant International Women's Boxing Federation world bantamweight championship by beating Hoy.

Christina Ruiz won the vacant International Female Boxers Association world bantamweight championship by beating an opponent who had one win in seven fights.

Katy Wilson Castillo has won multiple belts. So has Yazmin Rivas, who includes the WBC World Female bantamweight, WBC World Female super-bantamweight, and WBC Youth Female super-bantamweight titles among her baubles.

Alicia Ashley has also won multiple belts, including the WBC World Female super-bantamweight title.

And Monica Lovato once held the International Boxing Association female bantamweight championship. Thereafter, she won the NABF female super-lightweight championship by beating Crystal Hoy.

In sum, there's even less quality control as to who qualifies for a women's championship fight these days than there is for the men.

That brings us to Heather Hardy vs. Hoy.

Hardy's 10-and-0 record was deceiving. Most of her opponents have been mediocre. In her most recent bout, against Jackie Trivilino (9 wins in 19 fights), she was clearly outboxed. But judges Tony Paolillo and Waleska Roldan gave Hardy the nod, provoking a loud chorus of boos from the crowd. That dissent was particularly notable given the fact that the fight was contested at Barclays Center in Hardy's hometown of Brooklyn.

Hoy was a safe opponent for Hardy. Chrystal is an arm-puncher who plods straight forward in a one-dimensional attack with no power and is there to be hit. From round one on, it was clear that neither Hardy nor Hoy had the power to knock the other out and that, absent a cut or fluke injury, the bout would go the distance.

Hardy gives her all every time out, but too often uses her face as her first line of defense. This time, she relied on her legs; circling, countering, and getting off first, all of which was made easier by the fact that Hoy appeared to not know how to cut off the ring. The action was brisk but also repetitive. The rounds blurred together.

Virtually everyone who watched Hardy-Hoy saw Heather as the clear winner. Ring judge Joe Pasquale might not have been watching. He scored the bout 95–95. The other two judges scored it for Hardy by 100–90 and 99–91 margins. One hopes for Heather's sake that someday she has a legitimate championship fight. This wasn't it.

Women boxers, like their male counterparts, are deserving of respect. There's an inherent lack of respect in taking a club fight and labeling it a contest for an international championship. It's disrespectful to women boxers who have become true champions as a matter of merit. And it tarnishes women's boxing by saying to the public, "These are our champions. They're the best we have."

I was in Jermain Taylor's dressing room in the hours before and after his two victories over Bernard Hopkins in 2005. Those night are among the most memorable experiences that I've had in boxing, so later events have had a particularly poignant feel for me.

Jermain Taylor's "Comeback"

There was a time when Jermain Taylor was one of my favorite fighters, in and out of the ring. In his glory years, he fought Bernard Hopkins twice and beat him both times. The fights were close. The decisions could have gone either way; particularly in their first outing. But no one disputes the notion that Taylor tested Hopkins in ways that no one other than Roy Jones had tested Bernard before.

Then things turned sour for Taylor. Listening to the wrong people, he dumped trainer Pat Burns (who'd taken him from his first pro fight to the undisputed middleweight championship of the world). In 2007, after three lethargic title defenses, Jermain was knocked out by Kelly Pavlik. That ushered in a two-year period in which his ring ledger showed four losses in five fights, including three brutal knockout defeats and a brain bleed that Taylor suffered at the hands of Arthur Abraham in the opening round of Showtime's 168-pound tournament.

Taylor withdrew from the "Super Six" tournament after his loss to Abraham and spent the next two years away from the ring. During that time, his weight rose to over two hundred pounds. There were issues with drinking and women and run-ins with the law that seemed to result from stupidity rather than malicious intent. Pat Burns (who never lost his fondness for Jermain) put the matter in perspective, saying, "He's furious at the people who he now knows exploited him. And it spills over into how he feels about the rest of the world."

In December 2011, Taylor returned to the ring. He needed that structure in his life and he needed the money. Burns agreed to train him. Over the next two years, Jermain won four fights against club-fight-level opposition, raising his record to 32 wins, 4 losses, and 1 draw.

Then, on May 31, 2014, Sam Soliman of Australia won the IBF 160-pound belt by decisioning a shopworn Felix Sturm. That set the wheels of cynicism into high gear. Taylor's manager (the ubiquitous Al Haymon) arranged for third parties to pay an outsized purse to Soliman to defend his belt against Taylor. It was an investment; part of an effort by Haymon to wrest control another 160-pound weight class bauble.

Soliman was the ideal beltholder for a diminished Taylor to challenge. The Aussie is one month shy of his forty-first birthday and had lost eleven times. He's also a light puncher with only 18 knockouts to his credit in 56 fights.

Soliman-Taylor was slated for October 8, 2014, at the Beau Rivage Resort & Casino in Biloxi, Mississippi. Media reaction to the proposed fight was largely negative.

First, there was a school of thought that Taylor didn't deserve a title shot. He hadn't fought at 160 pounds since 2007 and hadn't beaten a world-class middleweight (as opposed to a blown-up super-welterweight) since 2005.

Second, although Jermain passed a battery of tests at the Mayo Clinic and Lou Ruvo Center for Brain Health, his prior brain bleed was cause for concern. Team Taylor said that Jermain was at no greater risk for injury than any other fighter. A number of doctors, including Margaret Goodman (former chief ringside physician for the Nevada State Athletic Commission and a foremost advocate for fighter safety) disagreed.

And there was another particularly troubling issue.

On August 26, Taylor was arrested at his home in Maumelle (a suburb of Little Rock) and charged with two felonies—first-degree domestic battery and aggravated assault—after shooting his cousin in the leg.

Lieutenant Carl Minden of the Pulaski County sheriff's office issued a statement to the media recounting the incident as follows: "Mr. Taylor's cousin and another individual came to his residence, and there was some sort of altercation. At some point, Mr. Taylor retrieved a handgun and fired several rounds. His cousin was struck multiple times. The cousin is alive and in serious condition at an area hospital."

Minden further stated that, when the police arrived at Taylor's home, Jermain was "very cooperative with our investigators. He was very calm, and there were absolutely no difficulties."

Piecing together information from multiple sources, it appears as though Taylor and his cousin had been at odds, a situation that was exacerbated when the cousin borrowed Jermain's truck and damaged it in a traffic accident. On the night of the shooting, the cousin appeared uninvited at Taylor's home with a second man (who a source says had recently been released from jail). Jermain ordered them off his property. They wouldn't leave, so Erika Taylor (Jermain's wife) called the police. Meanwhile, Jermain took a gun and fired some warning shots in the air, at which point the cousin said that Jermain didn't have the guts to shoot him. Taylor, who may well have felt physically threatened by then, shot his cousin three times in the leg.

One day after his arrest, Taylor was released on $25,000 bail. The court allowed him to leave Arkansas to train in Florida and fight Soliman in Mississippi.

Under the law, there's a presumption of innocence until proven guilty. That said; if Taylor had been playing in the National Football League, it's unlikely that he would have suited up on October 8. Further by way of analogy, Michael Phelps was arrested in Maryland on September 30 on suspicion of driving under the influence of alcohol. One week later, USA Swimming suspended him from competition for six months.

When fight night arrived, Taylor vs. Soliman was a sloppy ugly mess. Jermain fought tentatively and looked older than his thirty-six years. His timing was off and his punches had no pop. He looked like damaged goods. Fortunately for him, Soliman *was* damaged goods. The Aussie had hurt his right knee in training and acknowledged after the bout that he'd almost pulled out of the fight. He should have. It would have spared fight fans twelve horrible rounds of boxing.

People who were channel surfing and tuned in to Taylor-Soliman without the audio could have been forgiven for thinking that they were watching two club fighters in a walkout bout. Virtually no clean punches were landed, nor was there much effective aggression or ring generalship. As the rounds dragged on, Soliman's damaged knee became more and more of an impediment. He kept falling down, occasionally helped on his journey to the canvas by a jab or glancing blow from Taylor. Neither the referee, the ring doctor, or Soliman's corner had enough sense to stop the nonsense. And Jermain was unable to end it.

Taylor won a unanimous decision. Neither fighter would last three rounds against Gennady Golovkin. Of course, neither Soliman nor the current version of Jermain Taylor would have lasted three rounds against Taylor in his prime.

That brings to mind the thoughts of Pat English, who, at the start of Taylor's comeback, declared, "As one of the attorneys who litigated the Stephan Johnson wrongful death case, this is extremely troubling to me. These people are taking a boxer with all the classic symptoms of being 'shot' and who has had a brain bleed and allowing him to come back. This is a disaster waiting to happen. Stephan Johnson died after being allowed to fight after suffering what the scans showed to be a likely brain bleed. Do we want to repeat that?"

One might add that medical tests aren't the only indicator of when a fighter should retire. Just because a boxer passes a "head test" doesn't mean that he should be in the ring. Muhammad Ali received a clean bill of health from the Mayo Clinic before he fought Larry Holmes. There comes a time when the dangers inherent in boxing outweigh the benefits to be gained from fighting.

Meanwhile, Jermain Taylor will soldier on.

"It wasn't pretty," Pat Burns said ten hours after Taylor-Soliman. "But Jermain won. He's the guy getting on the plane and going home with the belt."

And as for Jermain's personal future?

"I think he'll be okay," Burns answered after a moment's reflection. "I hope he'll be okay. But it's hard to tell."

Bernard Hopkins was "old" by boxing standards when he knocked out Felix Trinidad in 2001 to claim the undisputed middleweight championship of the world. It was unthinkable back then that he would still be an elite fighter in 2014.

Hopkins-Kovalev: A Legacy Fight

The November 8, 2014, title-unification bout between Bernard Hopkins and Sergey Kovalev is shaping up as the most intriguing fight of the year.

Boxing is a young man's sport. Hopkins, now forty-nine, has redefined the age at which a fighter can perform at an elite level. The only parallels that come to mind are hockey great Gordie Howe (who played in all eighty games of the 1979 National Hockey League season at age fifty-one) and George Blanda (who played in every game for the 1975 Oakland Raiders, including the AFC championship game against the Pittsburgh Steelers, at age forty-eight). Several jockeys have also excelled at an advanced age, most notably Willie Shoemaker (who won the Kentucky Derby at age fifty-four).

When Hopkins enters the ring to face Kovalev, he'll be two months shy of his fiftieth birthday. Each step that he takes now is into uncharted territory.

"There are seasons in sports for an athlete's career," Bernard says. "I bloomed late. The candle burns out for all of us. I know that. The question is when. I'm forty-nine years old, and you still don't hear anybody saying, 'Bernard, get out of the game before you hurt yourself.' What does that tell you?"

"Let's talk about Father Time," Hopkins continues. "He's a son of a bitch. Father Time is undefeated. That's a fight I can't win and nobody on this earth can win. But I'll have to get beat up to know that it's time to go. Why should I talk about when I'll quit? That's like talking about dying when you're not sick."

Hopkins has remarkable genetic gifts. But the key to his success is that he has kept his discipline and focus for more than two decades. He's always in shape and rarely walks around at more than a few pounds above his fighting weight.

"You talk boxing. I live boxing," Bernard told the media at a press conference earlier this year. "I pay a price to be great. I've never just gone through the motions; not in training and not in a fight. Especially not just in a fight. If a fighter is just going through the motions in the ring, even if it's just for a second, he's at risk. It's like, if you're driving a car and not paying attention; one second is all it takes. One thing we know about boxing is, one punch can knock you out."

Sergey Kovalev, age thirty-one, was born in Russia. He started boxing at age eleven and compiled a 195-and-18 amateur record. His professional ledger stands at 25 wins and 1 draw with 23 knockouts. The draw is deceiving. It came three years ago against a fleeing Grover Young, who stopped long enough to claim that he'd been hit behind the head and was unable to continue. Under California rules, the contest went into the record book as a two-round technical draw.

In Kovalev's next fight, on December 5, 2011, he knocked out Roman Simakov. Three days later, Simakov died from a brain injury suffered during the bout. Since then, Sergey has had eight fights and won them all by knockout. When asked about Simakov's death by Chris Mannix of *Sports Illustrated*, Kovalev responded, "I am professional fighter. I cannot be concerned about these things."

When Kovalev smiles, he looks like a great white shark.

Hopkins holds the WBA and IBF 175-pound titles. Kovalev is the reigning WBO light-heavyweight champion. Sergey was tentatively slated to fight Adonis Stevenson (the WBC 175-pound beltholder) this autumn. But Stevenson ran like Usain Bolt from that fight and, later, from a proposed match-up against Hopkins. Thus, Hopkins and Kovalev signed to fight each other.

"You will agree that this caught a lot of people off-guard, wouldn't you?" Hopkins asked Rick Reeno of BoxingScene.com one day after the fight was signed.

It certainly did. Among the surprised was Kovalev, who declared, "It is a big fight, interesting fight. I was surprised he said yes. It is one of my dreams to fight him."

Give Hopkins credit. At age forty-nine, he's doing what Floyd Mayweather has refused to do. He's seeking out the most dangerous, fan-friendly opponent he can find. That says a lot about Bernard's championship pedigree. Indeed, looking back over the course of his career, it's hard to find a legitimate challenger who he has ducked.

"If you call yourself the best," Hopkins says, "then fight the best opponent that's out there. I don't run away from the fire. I run to it."

Signing to fight Kovalev shows how serious Hopkins is about wanting to pile more bricks onto the building that is his legacy. Hopkins-Kovalev has the potential to be a historically significant fight. If Bernard wins, it will burnish his record in a remarkable way. And if Kovalev wins, it could mark his emergence as an elite fighter.

The betting line opened with Kovalev as a 2-to-1 favorite. Hopkins plays down that fact, noting, "A lot of guys have been the favorite over Bernard Hopkins. The people who make the odds are not boxing people. They are people that set the odds so you can bet. I've proven them wrong more than they've proven me wrong."

John David Jackson, who has trained Kovalev for two years, knows Hopkins well. Jackson served in Bernard's camp as an assistant trainer for four years. Less pleasing for him to remember is the night of April 19, 1997, when Hopkins successfully defended his IBF middleweight crown in Shreveport, Louisiana, by knocking out John David in the seventh round.

"The key to beating Bernard is to make him fight the whole fight," Jackson says. "Take advantage of his age. Wear him down. Guys say that, and then they don't do it because, when they hit Bernard, he hits them back and they figure they'll wait a while longer before they go after him. But when Bernard hits you back is when he's most vulnerable. That's when you have the opportunity to trade punches with him."

In response, Hopkins says simply, "John David Jackson had his chance. John David Jackson got knocked out. So, to me, how can a teacher teach a student and the teacher flunked the test?"

In recent years, there has been a tendency to give Hopkins more credit for being old than for being good. That sells Bernard short. The foundation of his success is technique. Yes, his reflexes have slowed a bit. His legs aren't what they once were. And Hopkins himself acknowledges, "The body absorbs punches differently at age forty-nine that it does at thirty-five. When you get older, the punches hurt more and last longer."

But Hopkins has made up for these deficits with an ever-increasing mastery of timing, spacing, and angles. He has never been cut. His chin ranks with the best in the business. And in the ring, he controls his emotions as well as any fighter ever.

There's a report, confirmed by Abel Sanchez (who was present) and others who have seen a video, that Gennady Golovkin put Kovalev on the canvas with a body shot when the two men sparred with each other in Big Bear several years ago. Kovalev threw a right hand that was harder than Golovkin thought it should have been, and Gennady went after him. Sergey went down hard.

Hopkins has been known to hook hard to the body.

The fighters who have given Hopkins the most trouble over the years—Roy Jones, Jermain Taylor, Joe Calzaghe, and Chad Dawson—did it with speed. Kovalev is a relatively slow fighter.

And perhaps most significantly, Hopkins has gone twelve rounds in fifteen of his last sixteen fights. Kovalev has gone eight rounds once. In his entire career, Sergey has fought a full three rounds or more on only five occasions.

"I'm not worried about twelve rounds," Kovalev says. "I will prepare for it. I will be in physical shape. And more important, my head will be ready."

It sounds odd for a man just shy of his fiftieth birthday to key his strategy to coming on strong late in a fight. But against Kovalev, Hopkins might do just that. To boxing insiders, this is an even-money fight.

Hopkins will be the toughest opponent that Kovalev has faced to date. Nathan Cleverly and Ismayl Sillah (the previous "names" on Sergey's ledger) are hardly the second coming of Bob Foster and Archie Moore. Indeed, some insiders who have hailed Kovalev as the future of the light-heavyweight division are now hedging their bets, saying that, despite Sergey's power, he might be "tailor-made for Hopkins."

If Kovalev is tailor-made for Hopkins, what does that say about Hopkins? Sergey certainly doesn't seem to be "tailor-made" for any other light-heavyweight.

"Kovalev is coming to the fight with one bullet, and that's his punching power," Hopkins says. "Let him take his shot. I'm not going to run from the gun. I'm going to disarm him. I'm going to take away his big punch. This fight will be as easy for me as beating Kelly Pavlik. On November 8, you're gonna watch artwork. Enjoy the artwork. Enjoy the jazz that will be played amongst the breeze in the air at Boardwalk Hall. The concert is going to be great."

How will Hopkins-Kovalev play out? For now, let's give the final word to Don Turner.

Turner came to New York in 1959 and, the following year, was hired as a twenty-year-old sparring partner for Sugar Ray Robinson. Later, he became a trainer.

Turner was in Evander Holyfield's corner for both Holyfield-Tyson fights and with Larry Holmes when Holmes conquered Ray Mercer. He was also Kovalev's trainer for a brief period of time, and will be in Sergey's corner for Hopkins-Kovalev.

"It's going to be a tough fight," Turner says. "But Sergey is up for it. He really wants it. And Bernard has never fought anyone who hits as hard as Sergey hits. If Sergey throws one punch at a time, he'll have a problem. But if Sergey throws punches in combination like he can, it will be Bernard that has the problem."

"When Sergey gets hit," Turner continues, "he comes right back at you. He's as hungry as Bernard is. He just doesn't talk about it like Bernard does. And Sergey is mean. He's the meanest fighter inside the ring that I've seen since Carlos Monzon. He's a vicious puncher. He's not scared of anyone. And I'll tell you something else. When Bernard looks into Sergey's eyes just before they start the fight, he'll see a man that's just as hard as he is. Sergey killed a guy in a fight. Most fighters, if they're involved in something like that, they come back and maybe they take a little off their punches. Sergey came back meaner than before. Sergey has knocked out every guy he's fought since then. Think about that. Bernard will. Don't you think it will be on Bernard's mind when they get in the ring that Sergey killed a guy in a fight?"

Bernard Hopkins might not be able to beat elite fighters anymore.

A Look Back At Hopkins–Kovalev

November 8, 2014.

Boardwalk Hall in Atlantic City, touching the Atlantic Ocean.

Bernard Hopkins vs. Sergey Kovalev.

Given the dominant role that Hopkins's age played in the promotion, one might have thought of the event as "The Old Man and the Sea."

Hopkins's accomplishments are different from those of any fighter who has come before him. His hairline has receded. There's a lot of gray in his beard. Two months shy of his fiftieth birthday, he still moves like an elite athlete in and out of the ring. No other fighter has performed as well at such at advanced age.

Hopkins is passionate about Hopkins and one of the best self-promoters in boxing. During an October 21 media conference call, he declared, "I just want to make sure that, when there is debate about Bernard Hopkins's legacy, people will be up all hours of the night debating arguments on trying to figure out where we put this. Or do we start this new label with Bernard at the top and anybody else that comes after that underneath. To me, the best fighter ever is Sugar Ray Robinson. The best fighter after that is Muhammad Ali. Then the debate starts."

If one is ranking fighters on the basis of how they performed in their mid-to-late forties, Hopkins is on the short list above George Foreman and Archie Moore. He's a master of psychological warfare. "Psychological warfare, you will never win against me," Bernard says. But he's quick to add, "I don't look at my victories as getting in somebody's head. I look at it as being the better fighter, better plan, better preparation, and I took care of my business."

Taking care of business results from superb genetic gifts ("God-given physical ability"), dedicated preparation ("I've never gotten bored with boxing"), a great boxing mind ("No one studies his opponent and understands his opponent more than I do"), and an understanding of one's limitations ("Everybody has weakness; even I. There is no perfect fighter, and there will never be").

Also, while Hopkins fights by the rules, the only rule for a prizefight in his world is that there are no rules unless the referee enforces them. In that regard, he has been known to push the envelope.

"In most of Bernard's fights," Paulie Malignaggi notes, "Bernard ends up being the referee."

Not everyone appreciates Hopkins's style of fighting, which involves shutting down an opponent's offense through tactics that are aesthetically unpleasing to many fans. Jimmy Tobin expressed that dissatisfaction, writing, "Hopkins's fights have become a chore to watch, though saying as much is liable to have you branded a simpleton for failing to appreciate the nuance of noogies."

Meanwhile, Hopkins has compensated for the perceived lack of action in his fights by marketing himself as "The Executioner" . . . "B-Hop" . . . and most recently . . . "The Alien." Perhaps in his next incarnation, he'll call himself "The Easter Bunny."

The evaluation and marketing of Hopkins always comes back to his age. "This doesn't happen the way it's happening for me at this particular time in my life," he said recently. "Just enjoy it, understand it, and realize that you might not be alive to see it again."

The other side of the coin is the nagging question of what Bernard's success says about the current state of boxing.

"What if Michael Jordan came back tomorrow," Bart Barry writes, "and won an NBA championship? It would be a massive event, an orgy of media celebration, as one of the world's most famous athletes returned to a field of glory and dominated at an age that was absurd. But once the orgy got tired and broke up, what would it say about professional basketball that a man in his sixth decade [Jordan is fifty-one] was able to dominate the best professionals in their twenties? Were Michael Jordan still able to ply his craftsmanship and win titles outclassing LeBron James and friends in championship games, the NBA would know there was something dreadfully wrong with its product."

Friend and foe alike realize that there's something dreadfully wrong now with boxing. The best rarely fight the best. Boxers sometimes win "world championships" without championship skills and without ever having fought a world-class fighter.

Thus, on the plus side of the ledger for Bernard, Barry continues, "Hopkins is an embarrassment for most of his prizefighting countrymen, showing at age forty-nine a willingness to fail that few of today's best American fighters have shown since their bouts got computer-matched in the amateurs. The fight that best represents our sport in 2014 is one in which a man nearing his fiftieth birthday is challenging and imperiling himself more than any of our standard bearers in their primes."

The man Hopkins chose to fight to solidify his legacy was Sergey Kovalev.

Kovalev came out of the Russian amateur boxing system. It has been said that he had a working relationship with some of the less savory elements in Russian society at an earlier time in his life. Of course, Hopkins wasn't a choirboy when he was young either.

At the start of his pro career, Kovalev relocated to the United States under the guidance of manager Egis Klimas. He now lives in Florida with his wife and newly born son. His English is rapidly improving but is constricted by a limited vocabulary.

Sergey enjoys basic pleasures. "I like nice cars," he says. "I like to travel. I like action. Fishing is too slow for me; too much waiting. I love to drive fast, but I don't love speeding tickets for driving too fast. Friendship is important to me. I love my family. I miss my family and friends who are still in Russia."

He loves animals. In 2011, Kovalev adopted a three-month old Yorkshire terrier named Picasso. One year later, Picasso jumped out of a moving car and was killed on the road. Sergey still carries a photo of himself with Picasso on his smart phone.

Kovalev has a direct matter-of-fact approach to boxing. Answering a question on a media conference call, he acknowledged the possibility that he could lose to Hopkins. When pressed by a reporter who followed up with, "Are you not one hundred percent certain that you're going to beat Hopkins?" Sergey answered, "This is boxing. I can repeat for you, special for you, this is boxing and everything in boxing can happen. This is not swimming. This is not cycling. This is not running. This is boxing."

In private, Kovalev was more expansive, saying, "The fans, the media; they don't know what it is to be a fighter because they have never been punched in the face by a fighter. I feel fear. I am not a target. I don't like to get hit. In boxing, any punch from your opponent can be the last for you. It is very dangerous. I knew Magomed Abdusalamov from the national team in Russia. He was a friend; not my best friend, but a friend. I don't ever want to be like he is today."

In recent years, Atlantic City has fallen on hard times. Gambling revenue has dropped by roughly 50 percent since peaking at $5.2 billion in 2006. Trump Plaza, Revel, and Showboat closed their doors in 2014. Trump Taj Mahal might follow suit in the near future.

Still, there was a nice buzz for Hopkins-Kovalev with Bernard carrying much of the promotional load.

"I am fighter," Kovalev had said at the kick-off press conference in New York. "My English is poor. But I am sure that Bernard will talk enough to promote the fight for both of us." Thereafter, Sergey informed the media, "Bernard talks and fights. I just fight. Say and do are two different things." Kovalev also indicated that, given his limited English, he understood only about 10 percent of what Hopkins said.

"None of Bernard's talk will bother Sergey," Don Turner (Kovalev's first trainer in the United States and now a fight-week assistant to trainer John David Jackson) observed. "If I had a fighter and talk was bothering him, I'd tell my fighter to find another job."

One thing that did bother Team Kovalev though, was Hopkins's penchant for skirting the rules, conning referees, and fouling during fights.

"He can cut you from the head, from the elbow, from any part of his body," Sergey noted. "I hope and I wish that this fight will be very clean and fair. But any way I need to get a victory, dirty fight or clean fight, for me it doesn't matter. I am going to fight a clean fight, but I will fight dirty if Hopkins will fight dirty."

"Sergey says he wants a fair fight," Hopkins responded at the final pre-fight press conference. "You're the Krusher. Make your own fair fight."

The oddsmakers thought that Kovalev would do just that; a belief based in large measure on his high knockout percentage. Hopkins acknowledged his adversary's power, saying, "I have the same thoughts on Kovalev that most people do. He's a dangerous puncher. He has a 90 percent knockout rate. If he can punch like everyone says he can punch, there might not be a second chance."

Still, Bernard voiced confidence in the outcome of the fight, declaring, "Kovalev only had to be one-dimensional because the guys he fought he knocked out. But now you're stepping up to a different level. You're stepping up to the professor, the teacher. You're stepping up into a different neighborhood. The other neighborhoods, you understood. But this neighborhood is kind of strange."

One day before the fight, Oscar De La Hoya (now Hopkins's promoter) offered a thought regarding the upcoming bout. "I fought Pernell Whitaker," Oscar said. "I fought Mayweather. I could hit them. But not one punch I threw against Hopkins landed the way I wanted it to land."

"This is one of those fights where the energy level before is crazy and everyone is saying either guy can win," Naazim Richardson (Hopkins's trainer) added. "And when it's over, people will be sitting around saying, 'Is that all Kovalev has?'"

"Kovalev has a good amateur background," Richardson continued. "He knows how to box. He's not just a puncher. But Kovalev has never been past eight rounds, and now he's fighting the master of twelve. How does Kovalev handle that? What happens if Kovalev can't hit Bernard the way he wants? What happens if Kovalev hits Bernard with his best shot and nothing happens? Kovalev punches hard. We know that. His power is real. But so was Tarver's power and Pavlik's power. And Tarver and Pavlik had knockouts over legitimate champions. Kovalev doesn't have that."

"I need to do what I do and do it very well," Kovalev said of his date with Hopkins.

"The sweet science is not based on only one thing you can do particularly well," Bernard countered.

Main Events and Golden Boy (which co-promoted the fight) had hoped for a crowd of ten thousand. The announced attendance of 8,545 fell short of that goal. There was a horrible two-hour stretch in the middle of the card that consisted of 114 minutes of waiting and six minutes of boxing. But anticipation ran high when Hopkins and Kovalev entered the ring.

Kovalev made his presence forcefully known two minutes into the bout when he maneuvered Hopkins into a corner and dropped him with a short straight right as Bernard was sliding out to his left. It was a flash knockdown. A clubbing right hand that landed high on Hopkins's head later in the stanza probably did more damage. But Sergey knew now that he had a working game plan.

Thereafter, Kovalev fought a patient measured fight, controlling the distance between the fighters in a way that Hopkins was always under pressure yet unable to hold and maul. It wasn't a fast pace. It never is for Hopkins, which usually benefits the older man. But here, the pace meant that Sergey (who had gone eight rounds only once in his career and fought a full three rounds only five times) was less likely to drown in the deep water of the late rounds.

A fighter's game plan sometimes changes as a fight goes on. Kovalev's didn't. Unlike most Hopkins opponents, he was able to contest the battle on his own terms. He was faster that Hopkins had thought he'd be. Or maybe Bernard was slower. One way to beat Kovalev is to get off first, hit him just hard enough to keep him off balance, and force Sergey to reset. Hopkins knew that. But at age forty-nine, he couldn't do it.

Kovalev jabbed effectively to the body throughout the bout and landed some good chopping right hands up top. John David Jackson said afterward that he would have liked his charge to have thrown more body punches during exchanges on the inside. That said; Sergey did damage with the body shots that he threw and also with blows to the biceps and shoulder.

There were rounds when Hopkins set traps in the hope the Kovalev would blunder into one of them, and other times when survival seemed uppermost in his mind. "When Bernard got hurt," Jackson noted, "he'd go into his shell, gather himself together for a few rounds, then try another attack."

There was drama in the fight in large measure because one of the combatants was Bernard Hopkins.

Then, in round twelve, the drama escalated. Everyone in the arena (including Hopkins) knew that Bernard needed his first knockout in ten years to win. He went for it. And got rocked in return. That led to some big exchanges and ended with Kovalev battering Hopkins around the ring while Bernard struggled courageously to stay on his feet until the final bell.

One could make an argument for giving round seven to Hopkins. Kovalev didn't do much in that stanza, and Bernard snapped Sergey's head back with two good right hands. Other than that, it was all Kovalev. The judges' scores were 120–107, 120–107, and 120–106. Kovalev outlanded Hopkins by a 166-to-65 margin. Bernard averaged a meager five punches landed per round.

After the fight, Hopkins handled his defeat with dignity and grace.

"Sergey is the real deal," he acknowledged at the post-fight press conference. "I felt like a middleweight in there with a cruiserweight. I had some success here and there, but I never got him off his game. He was the better man tonight."

There was also a bit of humor when a questioner asked if Hopkins would fight again.

"Asking me about fighting again now is like asking a woman who's just out of nine hours labor about having another baby," Bernard responded.

Three days later, Hopkins told Fox Sports that he planned on having at least one more fight. That would take him past age fifty in the ring.

Kovalev has a bright future ahead of him. Prior to fighting Hopkins, Sergey had declared, "I want to get some lessons from the professor of boxing. I want to get some experience from this fight that can make me better for another fight."

He achieved that goal and got the win. He's an exciting action fighter and the best light-heavyweight in the world. But before one gets too carried away with superlatives, let's not forget that the man Kovalev just beat is forty-nine years old. A remarkable forty-nine-year-old, but forty-nine just the same.

In recent years, Hopkins has alluded to retirement. "When I leave, you all are going to miss me," he told the media at a press conference last year. "Where else are you going to get these sound bites?" Then, on a more pensive note, Bernard added, "Boxing is always going to be here. That's just the way it is. Boxing will be here way after me and everyone else in it now is gone."

It's impossible to know with certainty what Hopkins will do next. He likes to steer his own ship and will continue to confound. When he joined Golden Boy in 2004, one would have been hard-pressed to find an observer who thought that his tenure with the company would outlast Richard Schaefer's. But here we are in 2014 and that eventuality has come to pass.

Prior to Hopkins-Kovalev, there was a lot of talk about Hopkins "punking out" if things went against him inside the ring. If Sergey was dominating, if Sergey was landing heavy blows, Bernard would fake an injury or instigate a disqualification rather than go out on his shield.

That didn't happen. In round twelve, Hopkins was in extremis, unable to fully control his mind and body, facing the onslaught of a devastating puncher. In those perilous moments, Bernard didn't look for a way out. He put everything on the line and fought with the courage and heart of a champion.

If round twelve of Hopkins-Kovalev turns out to have been the final round of the remarkable ring career of Bernard Hopkins, it would be a good round on which to end.

"If you hit me in the face," Larry Holmes has said, "you better know how to fight because I'm going to hit you back."

Larry Holmes at Ecco

At five o'clock on December 6, 2014, Larry Holmes walked into Ecco, a popular Italian restaurant in downtown Manhattan. Holmes was in New York to attend the Shadow Box Film Festival, where a documentary about his life entitled *In The Arena* would be screened that night.

Holmes is regarded by most experts as worthy of a place on the short list of great heavyweight champions. One way or another, he found a way to beat people up.

The legendary trainer, Ray Arcel, who worked with Holmes late in their respective careers, once observed, "Larry had it all in the ring. The one thing he seemed low on was self-confidence. I always had to give him a kick to make him realize how good he was. I think some of that came from the fact that Don King kept him around for so long as Muhammad Ali's sparring partner. He was looked at for so long as just the warm-up guy that he never really developed the sense of pride and confidence and feeling of belonging that a fighter needs. I had to keep telling him, 'You're going to be long retired before people realize what a great fighter you are.'"

"I became a more determined fighter when I left Ali," Holmes says today.

That determination showed in the ring again and again, but never more notably than on September 28, 1979, when Earnie Shavers—who hit as hard as anyone in the history of boxing—left Holmes for dead on the canvas in round seven after landing a crushing overhand right.

"Holmes went down with a finality one does not often see, not even in the movies," Carlo Rotella wrote of that moment. "It looked like he had been shot with a tranquilizer dart just as he stepped on a land mine. I have never seen a man go down harder in a fight that he ended up winning."

But Holmes got up and won every round other than the seventh. He knocked Shavers out in round eleven.

"First, you get up," Larry explained afterward. "Then you worry about whether or not you're all right."

Holmes believes that the best he ever was as a fighter was on June 9, 1978, when he decisioned Ken Norton to claim the heavyweight throne. The fight that means the most to him was his June 11, 1982, victory over Gerry Cooney. Sandwiched in between those conquests was his October 2, 1980, execution of Muhammad Ali.

"Larry Holmes has shot Santa Claus," Jim Murray wrote afterward.

At Ecco, Holmes was comfortably dressed in a sport jacket and slacks. Several years ago when he was dining at Gallagher's Steak House, a fan had approached and complimented, "Larry; you're looking good."

"No, I'm not," Holmes countered. "I'm fat."

He has shed some pounds since then. And his life is good.

Larry and his wife have lived in the same comfortable house in Easton, Pennsylvania, for thirty-four years. When Holmes fought, he bought real estate, not bling. There was a time when he had considerable real estate holdings. Lately, he has been downsizing. An office building, a hotel, and the building in which the courthouse in Easton is lodged have all been sold. Holmes's last commercial real estate holding is his restaurant, Champ's Corner, which he plans to sell in the near future. He makes about fifty paid personal appearances a year and works a room well. He also co-hosts a cable-TV show entitled *What the Heck Were They Thinking* that's distributed in the Lehigh Valley area.

"People always criticized me when I fought," Larry says. "Now, on my TV show, I can criticize other people."

Among the words of wisdom that Holmes offered at Ecco were:

★ "I never wanted to be like Muhammad Ali. I wanted to be like Larry Holmes. I wanted to do my own thing, and I did."

★ "I learned from Ali. The most important thing I learned from him about boxing was how to move in the ring. I improved my footwork by sparring with Ali. But I'll be honest, I liked hanging out with Joe [Frazier] better. Joe sang; he danced. We'd talk about everything. Joe was more fun."

★ "I always I told the truth as I saw it. I still do. That the way I am. Some people don't like it, but I call things the way I see them. If I'm wrong, I can say I'm sorry afterwards."

★ "All these athletes and celebrities and other people who force themselves on women; there's no excuse for that. 'No' means no. Anybody can understand that. 'No' is the first word you learn after 'mama' and 'dada.'"

★ I'm happy to be alive and well, and I'm sad for anyone who's not."

And there was one more vintage Larry Holmes thought.

"What's the best thing about being a fighter?" I asked.

"The best thing about being a fighter is making money," Holmes told me. "Why do football players play football? For the money. Why do basketball players play basketball? For the money. Why do baseball players play baseball? For the money. I didn't fight to entertain people. I fought to get paid. Nobody was allowed to punch me in my face for free."

"Suppose you could travel back in a time machine and fight any heavyweight champion in history. Who would you want to fight?"

"If the money is the same," Larry answered, "tell me which one is the worst fighter, and that's the guy I want to fight."

Non-Combatants

Paul Hoggatt was one of the people behind the scenes who made HBO Sports great.

Remembering Paul Hoggatt

Very few people know who Paul Hoggatt was, and that's a shame. Paul was an integral member of the HBO family when the network was known as "the heart and soul of boxing." He began working for the sports department in 1978. At the time of his death on July 14, 2012, he was the longest-serving employee of HBO Sports.

Paul was the A2 on HBO's boxing telecasts, an audio engineer who sat ringside before and during fights. The last show he worked was the first bout between Manny Pacquiao and Tim Bradley on June 9, 2012. Five weeks later, he was dead.

Paul's work embodied the principles of how a good television team is put together. A man of his ability and character shouldn't be forgotten. Thus, this article.

Paul Hoggatt was born in Colorado on August 5, 1954, and moved to Las Vegas in the early 1970s. John Slagle, who was his friend for four decades, recalls, "I met Paul at one of my first jobs. I was working for KLVX Channel 10 in Las Vegas as a runner. You'd call it a production assistant today. I saw this guy sweeping the studio floor, so I went over to introduce myself and asked, 'Are a runner?' It was Paul. And he answered, 'Oh' yeah. I run a lot.' I found out later that he was a cameraman. But the floor was dirty and he wanted it clean."

That was Paul. Co-workers and friends describe him as "a neat-freak . . . meticulous . . . a detail man . . . a perfectionist . . . very intense about his work." There was more than a little Felix Unger in him.

On paper, the A2's job on an HBO boxing telecast is to set up and maintain the audio equipment at ringside. That includes the announcers' microphones, their talk-back system, everyone's earpiece (including camera operators), and effects microphones for crowd noise, knockdown counts, ten-second warnings, and the bell. Audio cables and wires have to be properly installed, and each piece of equipment must be functioning perfectly to ensure that sound is transmitted seamlessly from ringside to the production truck.

"Paul loved being a soundman," Slagle says. "He was happy doing what he was doing. Once he became a soundman, that was it. He didn't want to move up the ladder anymore."

The technical area at ringside before a big fight is a challenging environment in which to set up equipment. But it was a world where Paul excelled.

Larry Merchant has spent the past four decades working in television. Reflecting on that time, he says, "It has always been amazing to me that we can go someplace and there's a couple of trucks with a bunch of cameras and wires, and we can use that stuff to send images and sounds all over the world. Paul was one of the guys who helped make that magic happen. He was a pro, and the way he did his job made it easy for the rest of us to do ours."

Randy Flick is the A1 on HBO's boxing telecasts. He sits in the truck on fight night and mixes the sound as events unfold.

"When I started working for HBO in 2000," Randy remembers "I was told about everyone on the crew. And then I was told, 'Paul is Paul.' He was one of the most sincere people I've ever known. Paul looked people in the eye when he talked with them. If he said 'hello', he meant it. If he complimented you on doing a job well, you knew you'd done it right."

"And I'll tell you something else," Flick continues. "I've worked with hundreds of audio people, and Paul had the best ears of anyone I've ever known. He could hear the faintest hum or buzz. We'd be testing a microphone and Paul would say, 'I hear something.' I couldn't hear it. But if I turned the monitor way up, there it was."

Shep Berkon worked for Paul as an audio assistant for ten years.

"When I started at HBO," Berkon reminisces, "I made a point of setting up quickly because there was so much equipment and there were so many things to do. Everything I set up functioned properly, but the copper wires might not have been coiled perfectly or something else might not have been precisely the way Paul thought it should be. Then, one day, Paul took me aside and said, 'Be kind to your copper.' That was how he felt about the equipment. 'Be kind to your copper.' He was very precise. He wanted everything done a certain way. When Paul was done setting up, every cable and wire was perfectly in place. And when a show was over; you know how it is. Everyone wants to get out of the arena and get something to eat or go back to their room or do whatever it is they're going to do that night. Paul wouldn't leave until every piece of equipment was packed up and stored where it should be."

"But Paul was so much more than an audio engineer," Shep continues. "I've never met a more caring person. You come into this world, and so many people get caught up in, 'I'm friendly with this big-name fighter or this important executive or this powerful promoter. Paul was never into that. But whenever HBO went to an arena we'd been to before, Paul knew the name of every janitor, every electrician, all the little people. If there was a break at ringside, instead of spending ten minutes checking his e-mail, Paul would spend those ten minutes talking with people."

Marc Payton, who directed HBO's boxing telecasts for three decades, recalls, "Paul was the best audio engineer I ever worked with, and I've worked with some great ones. He set the standard for what an A2 should be. I can't think of an audio issue we ever had that Paul couldn't solve. But Paul was more than an A2. If someone new joined the team, Paul was the first one to help him out. On fight night, he was HBO's ringside general. He knew everyone's job in addition to his own and scrutinized every last detail in the technical zone to make sure that everything was right."

Jim Lampley echoes Payton's thoughts, adding, "An A2 has the option of saying to himself, 'I'm going to put the microphones where they should be, see that everything is working, and wait until something goes wrong to fix it. Nowhere is it written that the A2 has to worry about someone walking behind the announcers when we're on camera, whether the production coordinator needs assistance, whether the ringside camera positions are secure. Paul made every bit of that and more his job. He went far above and beyond what an A2 normally does. He was always proactive in helping other people on the crew. He interfaced with arena security to make sure that HBO's arena positions were secure. That was a choice he made because he felt personally invested in the shows. And he was allowed to do what he did because of the enormous trust that everyone on the crew had in him."

"The people on the crew adored Paul," Lampley continues. "He was appreciative whenever someone did something nice for him and never took other people's kindness for granted. After every crew meal, he'd walk over and thank the servers. He had a huge influence on a generation of young production people at HBO. The only complaint I ever had about Paul was that it took me five years to get him to stop calling me 'Mr. Lampley.'"

"Paul was the ultimate team player," executive producer Rick Bernstein says. "He was never negative. He never had an agenda of his own. It was always about what was best for the team."

Will Hart (HBO's photographer at ringside) has similar memories and recalls, "Paul showed up early, set things up, looked out for everybody, and worked harder than anyone. He was the A2, but he really ran the entire technical zone for HBO. He was our hands-on guy in there. Whatever you needed, Paul made sure you got it. If you had any kind of technical issue, you went to Paul. He was always asking, 'What do you need? How can I help you?' He always made sure I had power for my computer. Everybody needs power. Everybody is screaming for power. And Paul facilitated getting power for everybody. That was largely because he was such a great guy. But the thought also crossed my mind that Paul was concerned I might plug into his audio rack on my own one night and screw up his system. Helping me get power was the surest way to head that off."

Paul was married and divorced twice. He didn't have children. He thought of himself as having two families. One was comprised of his co-workers at HBO. The other consisted of a few close friends.

Paul's best friend was Don Jacobs, who died in 2009. Don and his wife, Becky, had three sons: Dan, Jeff, and Greg. Paul spent most holidays with the Jacobs family.

Dan Jacobs now runs a small video production company in Las Vegas.

"Paul always treated people with respect," Dan says. "He was a good listener. When you were talking with Paul, you had his full attention. There was a warmth about him. He was more than kind; he was caring. And he was gentle. He literally wouldn't hurt a fly. There were times when I saw him catch an insect in our house and take it outside rather than kill it."

As for Paul's professional side, Dan says with a smile, "He was a sound man. He always told me, 'Don't forget the sound. If you have a picture of a waterfall, it goddamn well better sound like a waterfall.'"

Paul had his share of idiosyncrasies. One of them was that he wore a hardhat at ringside. That's because, once years ago, some arena workers had lowered a lighting truss to adjust it, and Paul whacked his head on the truss.

"He had his own personal HBO travel bag," Dan recalls. "It must have weighed seventy pounds. There were twenty rolls of tape, wrenches, a flashlight. You name it, and it was in there. Paul was better prepared than a Boy Scout."

The travel bag also contained three hardhats.

Paul smoked a lot. He ate the wrong foods and didn't take care of himself as well as he should have.

"He was very loving but also very elusive," John Slagle says. "He did his own thing."

"Paul's private life was his private life," Dan explains. "There were times when he lived a pretty wild life away from work, but that was his choice."

Paul lived alone in a small three-bedroom house.

"It looked brand new when he died," Dan says. "And he'd lived there for thirteen or fourteen years. The carpet was pristine. When you came in, you had to take your shoes off and Paul gave you booties to wear over your socks. He didn't want to put nails in the walls, so he never hung pictures. They were just propped up on the floor, leaning against the walls. There was very little furniture. Everything was in its place. Every piece of clothing was folded perfectly or hung just right."

In 2012, Paul began having digestive problems. And he was losing weight. He hated going to doctors. Finally he went. The diagnosis was colon cancer that had metastasized throughout his body. Paul was told that he had about six weeks to live. That didn't leave much time for wrapping things up. Denial, anger, bargaining, depression, and acceptance followed one another in quick progression. Paul went home, stayed there for a few weeks, and then went to Becky Jacobs's home for final hospice care.

When people know they're dying and don't have much time left, they often think about what they want to do with their remaining days.

I want to do this with my husband or wife. I want to take this trip with my children or revisit my boyhood home.

"Paul wanted to go back to work for one last telecast," Shep Berkon remembers. "It just wasn't possible. He couldn't walk. His body was withering away. But that's where his heart was."

Bill Chaikowsky, who worked on the ring apron for HBO as a handheld-cameraman for eighteen years, visited Paul the day before he died.

"You knew the end was near," Bill says. "Paul told me that he would have liked to have lived longer, but that he had made his peace with whatever was coming. He told me, 'I'm not afraid.'"

And Randy Flick (the man who had been informed on his first day of work that "Paul is Paul") discovered that Paul was still Paul.

"When Paul found out he was dying," Randy remembers, "at first he didn't want anyone to visit him. Then he said it would be all right. I went over to see him at Becky's when I was in Las Vegas the day before a fight. He was all skin and bones by then. It was obvious that the end was near. But Paul was at peace with himself. And he was still a perfectionist. He said to me, 'You know, Randy, I've never had to die before.' He wanted to do it right."

"Almost two years have passed since Paul died," HBO producer Jon Crystal says. "And even now when I go to a fight, I have the feeling that someone important is missing. There are a lot of people who you like and you're sad when they die but you don't miss them. I miss Paul."

Paul was proud of his accomplishments as an audio engineer. But the personal relationships that he developed within the HBO family meant more to him than his work.

When George Foreman retired as an HBO commentator, he quietly gave gifts to a handful of people who occupied a special place in his heart. Paul was one of them. George gave Paul a gold pocketwatch.

"That was Paul's Emmy," HBO production manager Holly Peterman says. "He was very moved that George felt that way about him. Paul didn't tell many people about it because he was a private person, and he didn't want anyone else's feelings to be hurt. But George's gift meant a lot to him."

When Foreman remembers Paul today, the phrase that comes first to his mind is "consistent kindness." Then George tells a story that reveals a great deal about both men.

George had the habit before and during telecasts of twisting the cord to his headset around his fingers.

"Please don't wrap it around your fingers," Paul pled on more than one occasion.

"But Paul saw this was going to be a problem," George recalls. "So one time, he brought me a long string with knots to keep me occupied. And for each fight after that, he brought me another."

Foreman has a case with what he calls "precious keepsakes" at his home in Texas. There's no title belt in the case. But one of the things in it is the last "long string with knots" given to him by Paul Hoggatt.

Whenever I research a major article about boxing, Don Turner is one of my go-to guys.

Don Turner: Opinions and Memories

Don Turner is one of my favorite people in boxing. I met him in 1984 and have been learning from him ever since.

Turner grew up hard in Cincinnati. "I have no idea what my father did," he told me years ago. "We were on welfare and lived in the projects about four blocks from Ezzard Charles. In Cincinnati, boxing was a thing with most young guys. Boxing or basketball or track. I chose boxing because, when I was growing up, Ezzard Charles was one of the greatest fighters in the world."

Turner compiled a 4-and-2 amateur record and turned pro in 1959. In his pro debut, he lost a six-round decision to Stanley "Kitten" Hayward in Hayward's hometown of Philadelphia. That set a pattern for future fights. Turner would be brought in as the opponent for house fighters like Johnny Persol, Giulio Rinaldi, and Roger Rouse.

On occasion, he scored an upset. What was his biggest win as a fighter?

"I didn't have one," Turner acknowledged. "But if I had to choose, I'd say it was a decision over Ike White on the undercard of the first fight between Dick Tiger and Joey Giardello."

Turner retired from active ring duty in 1969 and began training fighters. In 1996, after Evander Holyfield upset Mike Tyson with Turner in his corner, the Boxing Writers Association of America honored Don as "Trainer of the Year." He also trained Larry Holmes for six years that included Holmes's upset victory over Ray Mercer.

When Sergey Kovalev came to the United States, Turner was his first trainer. He's still part of Team Kovalev and was in Atlantic City for the November 8, 2015, title-unification bout between Kovalev and Bernard Hopkins. On the night of November 7, Don and I had dinner together.

Turner has a lot of memories. As a twenty-year-old middleweight, he was hired to spar with Sugar Ray Robinson when the master was readying to defend his title against Paul Pender.

"Robinson sparred nine rounds a week," Turner recalled. "Three rounds on Monday, three on Wednesday, and three on Friday. Each round was with a different sparring partner, and each round was a war. The first day I sparred with him, the other two sparring partners were Otis Woodard [a veteran of thirty-seven pro fights] and Clarence Hinnant [who won forty bouts in a career that included a knockout victory over Yvon Durelle]. First round, Robinson knocks Woodard down. Second round, he knocks Hinnert flat. Now it's my turn. Robinson was old by then, but he could still fight. He hit me with a left hook that knocked my headgear clear out of the ring. I must have strapped it on wrong. But I stayed on my feet."

Turner has a lot of opinions and isn't shy about voicing them. There was a time not long ago when the representative of a well-known promoter was on site for a fight, clearly high, and giving Don a hard time.

"Tell him he's going to have to find a different way to do his cocaine," Turner advised an interested third party. "Because I'm going to break his nose."

Among the thoughts that Turner offered at dinner the night before Hopkins-Kovalev were:

★ "I think I'm a good trainer. And one reason I'm a good trainer is that I tell fighters the truth."

★ "The thing that bothers me the most about boxing today is that nobody feels guilty about anything wrong that they do. Nobody stands up for what's right anymore. They just pretend to."

★ "Too many fighters today do everything but what they're supposed to do. The partying is more important to them than the training. If they come to training camp and make weight, they think they had a good camp."

★ "In the old days, the trainer was in charge. Now you've got five people telling the fighter what to do. The strength and conditioning coach is telling the fighter one thing. His buddies and maybe his father are telling him something else. When Greg Popovich is coaching the San Antonio Spurs, he closes the door, and nobody's father and nobody's agent and nobody's friends come in. But fighters today listen to everybody."

★ "Most of the boxing writers today are just fans. They have no idea what they're writing about. You've got guys who don't know the first thing about boxing sitting behind a computer, writing this trainer did

this wrong and this fighter did that wrong. That's how stupid some boxing writers are."

    ★ "A fighter can't become world class without fighting other world
class fighters. These guys who don't fight anybody on the way up; finally,
they're in a big fight. And they look like a baseball player who hit sixty
home runs against minor league pitching and is coming up to the big
leagues for the first time. I don't judge a fighter until I've seen him in
trouble. And I judge fighters by who they fought. It's real simple. Who
did you beat?"

    And there was a final grace note:

    "Whatever you write about me, put in a word about Bobby
McQuillen. He knew as much about boxing and taught me more about
boxing than anyone ever. Bobby McQuillen, Bill Miller; guys like that
weren't as famous as the made-for-television trainers you have in boxing
today. But they were great boxing guys."

When John Duddy was asked by a reporter why he was retiring from boxing, he responded, "Have you seen my fights?" Now that Duddy is pursuing a career in acting, it doesn't bother him when someone—for example, a film director—looks at him and says "cut."

John Duddy: Actor

In 2011, John Duddy retired from boxing. Living in New York, the popular Derry native had compiled a 29-and-2 record with 18 knockouts. He'd experienced the thrill of fighting before cheering crowds in Madison Square Garden and also in his beloved Ireland.

Now, at age thirty-five, Duddy is pursuing a new career. He wants to be an actor.

There's a long tradition of boxers trying their hand at acting. In the 1880s, John L. Sullivan realized that, as heavyweight champion, he could make large amounts of money by appearing on stage in vaudeville and legitimate theatrical productions. James Corbett defeated Sullivan in 1892 and immediately embarked upon a theatrical career that was noteworthy for its longevity and success. Corbett began in vaudeville, made numerous forays into theater, and worked hard to develop his craft. Late in life, he appeared in feature films.

In the 1920s, Jack Dempsey signed a contract to star in ten Hollywood films for a million dollars. Muhammad Ali starred on Broadway in *Buck White*, appeared in a television mini-series entitled *Freedom Road,* and played himself in the feature film, *The Greatest*. Mike Tyson has landed several small film roles and starred in a one-man show on Broadway.

When Duddy was boxing, he was approached from time to time by entertainment types who suggested that he try his hand at acting. His response was always the same.

"Right now, I'm a fighter."

That changed in January 2011. John had been offered a six-figure purse to fight Andy Lee on HBO. Rather than accept the offer, he retired.

"I no longer have the enthusiasm and willingness to make the sacrifices that are necessary to honor the craft of prizefighting," Duddy said at the time. "I used to love going to the gym. Now it's a chore. I wish I still had the hunger, but I don't. The fire has burned out. And I know myself well enough to know that it won't return. It would be unfair to my fans, my trainer and manager, and everyone else involved in the promotion of my fights for me to continue boxing when I know that my heart isn't in it. I've always given one hundred percent in the gym and in my fights. I have too much respect for boxing and the people around me to continue fighting when I know that I can't do that anymore."

"Barry McGuigan was one of my childhood heroes," Duddy continued. "His photograph was one of the first things that visitors saw when entering our home in Derry. He had great influence on me when I was a boy. Barry McGuigan once said, 'Fighters are the first people to know when they should retire and the last to admit it.' I know that it's time for me to retire from boxing, and I'm admitting it. I give you my word; I will not come back."

Since then, Duddy has taken acting classes and participated in several workshops. His good looks and boyish charm are appealing. He had a scene in a Jon Bon Jovi music video, and was cast in the role of a young fighter in the play, *Kid Shamrock*. Now he's moving into more rarified terrain.

Thirty-five years ago, Robert DeNiro played Jake LaMotta in the Academy Award–winning film, *Raging Bull*. In 2013, DeNiro returned to the ring—this time, opposite Sylvester Stallone—in *Grudge Match*. He needed a trainer to prepare for the fight scenes, and Duddy got the nod.

"I was surprised by how fit DeNiro was," John says. "We hit if off, and I also got to know Robert Sale, who was responsible for choreographing the fight scenes. Sale told me what he wanted to have happen in the ring, and I did my best to get DeNiro ready to do it. The training lasted three-and-a-half weeks. When it was over, DeNiro said I could stay around, so I watched them work until they left New York to film in New Orleans."

Then opportunity struck.

In September 2013, Sale telephoned Duddy and told him, "You're going to get a call on your cell phone from a number you don't recognize. Answer it."

"I got the call," John recalls. "I answered it. And it was DeNiro. He was starring in a film called *Hands of Stone*, and the actor who was supposed to play Ken Buchanan had just pulled out. Did I want the role?"

Hands of Stone chronicles the career of the legendary Panamanian boxer, Roberto Duran, known to the world as "Manos de Piedra." DeNiro is cast as Ray Arcel, Duran's trainer. Edgar Ramirez plays Duran. Buchanan is the Scotsman whose two-year reign as lightweight champion ended in 1972, when he was dethroned by Duran at Madison Square Garden.

"Filming *Hands of Stone* was an incredible experience," Duddy says. "A lot of it, including the fight scenes that were supposed to be at Madison Square Garden, was filmed in Panama. Obviously, it was important in terms of my acting. But one of the things that meant the most to me was, I never saw Muhammad Ali train or fight. I never saw Sugar Ray Robinson train or fight. But now I've watched Robert DeNiro prepare for a role and then perform that role in front of the camera. That was very special for me."

Hands of Stone will be released in late 2015. It's anyone's guess where Duddy's acting career will go from there.

"I enjoy acting," John says. "Being onstage is a bit like boxing. You rehearse; you prepare. You go over your lines again and again until they're ingrained in your memory. At times, it's monotonous the same way that training for a fight and doing the same things in the gym again and again is monotonous. And when you're onstage in a play, like with boxing, there's an element of fear. There's no safety net. You're living in the moment. If something goes wrong, you have to fix it in a hurry. Films don't have the same element of danger, but I like films too."

Does Duddy miss boxing?

"No," John answers. "I'm glad I did it, and I'll never do it again. My goal when I started boxing was to become a world champion. That was my biggest motivation all those years. One of the reasons I retired was that I saw so many ex-champions who aren't doing well. Physically, mentally, they're having problems. I was getting into my thirties. I always got hit more than I should have as a fighter. And I realized that being a world champion wouldn't necessarily make me happy in the long run. Damage is a strong word. But in boxing, every time you fight, you lose a piece of yourself that you can never get back again. I didn't want to go on longer than I should. One of the things I love about acting is that, with each role, instead of being damaged, I'm adding to who I am. Even when I'm in a play and have the same role night after night, it's new every time. That's part of the fun."

So . . . In Duddy's fantasies, would he rather win an Academy Award for best actor or be the undisputed middleweight champion of the world?

"That's a damn hard question," John answers. "One would have been nice before. The other would be nice now. I hope I have a future in acting. But for the moment, I'm taking things one step at a time. I'd like to get a good agent. I'd like to be a working actor. But whatever happens, I've done some pretty cool things so far."

Curiosities

Sacking the quarterback is light punishment compared to a knockdown in boxing.

"I'm Going Down"

When Bernard Hopkins was dropped by Sergey Kovalev in round one of their title-unification bout in Atlantic City, it marked the third fight in which Hopkins visited the canvas.

Knockdowns in boxing vary widely in cause and effect. Some knockdowns result from glancing blows that land when a fighter is off balance. At the other end of the spectrum, sometimes a fighter gets whacked.

A fighter can be knocked down and suffer no adverse consequences other than embarrassment and the loss of a point. Or he can be hurt badly enough that he's unable to think clearly and fully control his motor skills.

Hopkins has experienced both ends of the spectrum. Jean Pascal knocked him down twice in their first encounter. In each instance, it was a flash knockdown. But there was a time when "Father Time" found himself in more dire circumstances.

"I remember it like it was yesterday," Hopkins recalls. "I was fighting Segundo Mercado in Ecuador [on December 17, 1994]. Fifth round, I didn't see the punch. He's punching and I'm punching and he got there first. I don't remember falling at all. That's how hard I got hit. I remember being on the canvas and asking, 'How did I get down here?' I got up. He knocked me down again in the seventh round, and the judges scored the fight a draw. Four months later, we fought again and I knocked him out."

Larry Holmes is remembered for rising from the canvas after being knocked woozy by Earnie Shavers and Renaldo Snipes and, in each instance, coming back to KO his opponent.

Holmes's philosophy with regard to being knocked down is simple: "First you get up. Then you worry about whether or not you're all right."

Some of boxing's other well-known practitioners have their own memories of being knocked down.

Roy Jones: "The big thing is, a knockdown is a loss of control. And a fighter never wants to lose control. The first time I got knocked down in

the pros, it was by Louie Del Valle [on July 18, 1998]. I don't remember
going down. It was like I blacked out for a second and then, 'Son of a
bitch knocked me down. Now I'm pissed.' I got up and won every round
in the fight except that round. And there were a couple of fights that you
know about where I got knocked down that were worse. That was the
same sort of blackout only longer. There's also the sort of knockdown
that happened in my last fight in Poland [against Pawel Glazewski on
June 30, 2012], which was a balance thing. I said to myself, 'Oh, shit; I'm
going down. I got to get up fast, so they don't think I'm hurt.'"

Mark Breland: "It was against Marlon Starling [on August 22, 1987].
I don't remember the punch. I was on the ropes and he hit me. As I was
going down, I said to myself, 'Oh, shit.' Then I hit the ground with a thud.
The feeling was almost like being relaxed. It was an awkward feeling. I
was telling myself to get up, but I couldn't. I thought I was getting up, but
I was more struggling than anything else. And then it was over."

Kevin Kelley: "The first time I got knocked down was by Gregorio
Vargas the night I won the featherweight title [December 4, 1993]. It was
like there was a flash and a pop. One moment, I was standing up. The
next moment, I was on the ground. I didn't even know I was falling. In
thirty-six fights, it had never happened before. But the thing is, after it
happens once, it plants a seed in your head and it can happen more easily
because you're more comfortable with the idea of getting knocked down.
I probably should have gone to counseling or therapy for it. Because after
that, when I got hit and hurt, something in me would choose to go
down rather than get hit again. Fighters think weird things. Thirty-six
professional fights, no knockdowns. And after that, I got knocked down
all the time."

Micky Ward: "I had pretty good balance, so there were no flash
knockdowns. Each time I went down, I was buzzed. I got knocked down
four or five times. Sometimes, it was like a light went dark for a second
in my head and I was down. Sometimes, I was aware that my equilibrium
was screwed up and I was stumbling. Each time, my first reaction was to
ask, 'How did I get here?' But you know how you got there. You got hit
hard in the head."

Randy Neuman: "I went down a couple of times from flash knock-downs. You go down; you get back up. It's not a big thing. The first time I was really hurt was by a guy named Jimmy Harris [on February 18, 1971]. He didn't know how to fight. I was playing with him and got careless. Then I found out that he could punch. A fighter isn't a good witness when he's knocked down like that because he doesn't remember everything. And if you saw what was happening as it unfolded, you wouldn't have gotten knocked down to begin with. For me, it was like the electricity was shut off in my brain. I got up before ten and I knew where I was. But I was out on my feet and the referee stopped it."

Zab Judah: "Knockdowns are about timing. Knowing how to get to the other guy faster and better than he gets to you. The first person to knock me down in the amateurs or pros was Jan Bergman [on February 12, 2000]. It was my first world title fight. I knocked him down twice in the first round. Second round, he hit me with a hook up top. I'd never been knocked down before, so I didn't realize what was happening. Then it was, 'Oh, no! I'm down.' It was a flash knockdown. I wasn't hurt. I was more embarrassed than anything else. I'm like, 'Damn! I can't change what happened now.' So I got up and did what I had to do to win the fight."

And then there's the Golden Boy, Oscar De La Hoya, who shared a remarkably candid recollection with this writer.

"I got knocked down four times in the pros," De La Hoya recalled. "The first time was by Narciso Valenzuela. He hit me square on the chin, but it was more a question of my being off-balance. I got up and knocked him out a minute later. The second time was pretty much the same thing against Giorgio Campanella. And Ike Quartey knocked me down with a left hook that was a good punch but also just a flash knockdown. I had good whiskers. Those knockdowns were more embarrassing to me than anything else. Each time, I said to myself, 'This shouldn't be happening to me. I'm a superior fighter.'"

"The other time I got knocked down," De La Hoya continues, "was by Bernard Hopkins. That's interesting because we're talking about the whole psychological aspect of where I was in my life at that time. The fight was competitive. I was in the fight. But it was a very unhappy time in my life. I was tired of being who I was. He hit me with a good body shot. I went down. I've asked myself a thousand times since then, 'Could I have gotten up?' And the answer is 'yes.' But I wanted everything to be over. Not the fight; being the Golden Boy, everything. It wasn't something I consciously thought out when the referee was counting. But those conflicts inside me caused me to stay down. You have to go really deep into the root to understand."

The continuing adventures of David Diamante.

David Diamante at Pamplona

Several years ago, I wrote, "The most conventional thing about David Diamante is his hair."

Diamante is the ring announcer with the stentorian voice who's instantly recognizable by dreadlocks that extend below his waist. He's also the in-arena voice of the NBA Brooklyn Nets. His most recent departure from convention led him to participate in one of the world's best-known spectacles. He ran with the bulls in Pamplona.

Pamplona is a city in northern Spain that was founded as a camp for Roman solders in 74 BC. Each year, the San Fermin Festival is held there from July 6 through July 14. The festival highlight is the running of the bulls, made famous by Ernest Hemingway in his 1927 novel *The Sun Also Rises*.

The bulls run each morning on the final eight days of the festival. Six bulls are let loose from a corral at one end of the course and rampage 900 yards through cordoned-off streets to a bull ring where they will die that afternoon.

The people who "run with the bulls" position themselves at various points along the route and run to the bullring ahead of the bulls. Barricades along the way keep the bulls on course but have openings wide enough for runners to slip through if they want out. Women have been allowed to participate since 1974, but virtually all of the runners are men.

Participants must be at least eighteen years old and are required to run in the same direction as the bulls. Most of the injuries sustained by runners involve cuts and bruises that result from falls. But dozens of runners are gored each year, a handful of them seriously. There have been fifteen deaths since 1924, the most recent occurring in 2009.

The obvious first question to ask Diamante was, "Are you out of your mind?"

"That's a fair question," David answered. "I'm not trying to get hurt. It's dangerous; I know that. But danger breeds excitement, and a big part of life is facing your fears and conquering them. I have faith in my courage, my intelligence, my quickness, and my physical strength. And I have a history of adventurous travel. Tibet, India, Somalia, Haiti, Honduras, the jungles of Colombia. When I was in Nicaragua, I met a guy who got in touch with me later and said, 'I'm going to Pamplona to run with the bulls. Do you want to come?' I told him, 'Count me in.' It was a calculated risk. Look; I ride a motorcycle every day in New York. If you do that on the Cross-Bronx Expressway with eighteen-wheelers on either side of you, what's a bull?"

Diamante ran with the bulls three times—on July 7, 8, and 10—before leaving Pamplona on the morning of July 11. He'd never been to a bullfight before, but went twice in Pamplona. Each time, all six bulls were killed.

"I'd be lying to you if I didn't admit to having reservations about bullfighting," Diamante acknowledges. "They don't fight the bulls until the age of five. Until then, the bull has a pretty good life; a lot better than the animals that are turned into the meat we eat. But no matter how you look at it, the bull is an unwilling participant in the fight. I'm not attacking what anyone else believes. I'm just speaking for me."

The running of the bulls in Pamplona starts at precisely 8:00 am, when a rocket is fired into the air and the bulls are released from their pen. They're big and they're angry.

Runners can position themselves anywhere on the course except within thirty yards of the pen. That gives the bulls a running start and the runners a chance to escape. Some runners start at the far end of the course where there's no danger.

"But let's be honest about it," Diamante says. "If you start off at the end of the course completely out of harm's way, you haven't really run with the bulls."

Diamante positioned himself as close as possible to the starting gate. By tradition, the runners wear red and white. He was wearing white pants, a white shirt, red scarf, red sash, and an old pair of running shoes. The balconies and windows overlooking the streets and the area behind the street barricades were lined with spectators.

"You'd be an idiot if you didn't feel some fear," Diamante says of the experience. "I had an uneasy feeling when I was waiting for the rocket to go off before the start of the run. If you're gored, the initial wound is only the start of your problems. You can be trampled by the bull and dragged along the street. But I can honestly say that, in the moment before the rocket went off, there was no place on earth that I would rather have been."

As for the run itself, there were moments of truth.

"The first day, I reached out and touched two bulls on the side as they ran past me," Diamante recalls. "That was exhilarating. In my mind, I wasn't running from the bulls. I was running with them. But it's dangerous, and the other runners are as big a danger as the bulls. You're running. There are people in front of you who slow you down. Sometimes they fall down, and you have to jump over them."

Diamante's moment of crisis came on the third day that he ran.

"There are so many people in the street," he says, "that sometimes there's nowhere to go. A bull came right at me. I knew I was in trouble. And I was gored. But fortunately, the point of the horn ran across my stomach rather than into it."

Ten days later, Diamante still had a bruise on his abdomen where the bull's horn had grazed him an inch above his navel.

"But each time I ran," he says, "I was walking on air afterward. The high I got from participating in one of the world's great traditions, testing myself, and the camaraderie I felt with the other runners is something I'll treasure for the rest of my life. Either you do this sort of thing or you don't. I do it."

Of course, Michael Buffer would have done it wearing dress shoes and a tuxedo.

Despite the ups and downs of life in and out of the ring, Manny Pacquiao remains a feel-good story.

Tina and Manny Redux

Millions of words have been written about the adoration that the Filipino people feel for Manny Pacquiao. Five years ago, I put a face on that adoration in the person of Tina Cruz.

Tina was born in the Philippines in Santiago Isabela province. Her parents were rice farmers. In 1983, she came to the United States. Five days a week, Tina rose at four o'clock in the morning and went to the design company in New York where she worked in cleaning maintenance. With Top Rank's permission, I brought her to Yankee Stadium to meet Manny at the kick-off press conference for his 2009 fight against Miguel Cotto.

Tina was ushered into a stadium restaurant that was closed to the outside world to meet Pacquiao before the proceedings began. They were introduced. Then the image she'd seen on television for years was talking with her. They spoke in Tagalog; about his children and hers, life in the Philippines, and her joy in meeting him. After the press conference, Manny posed for a photo with her and gave her autographs for several family members.

"Omigod!" Tina says, looking back on that day. "After that article about me and Manny, I got so many calls. Some of them were from people I hadn't seen for years. They were all asking, 'Did you really meet Manny?' I told them, 'Yes! And he was so nice. He really talked to me.'"

Tina turned seventy-five on September 4, 2014. That day, a press conference (the last stop on a six-city 27,273-mile media tour) was held at the Liberty Theatre in New York to promote the November 22 fight in Macau between Pacquiao and Chris Algieri. To celebrate Tina's birthday, once again I brought her to meet Manny.

In 1948, reflecting back on all that had happened to him as a consequence of boxing, Joe Louis observed, "I couldn't dream that big." The same might be said of Pacquiao.

Manny rose to iconic status after beating Oscar De La Hoya in 2008, one year before he and Tina met. A lot has happened since then.

After devastating Miguel Cotto, Pacquiao scored back-to-back triumphs at Cowboys Stadium over Joshua Clottey and Antonio Margarito. Victories over Shane Mosley and Juan Manuel Marquez followed. Then Manny lost a controversial decision to Tim Bradley and suffered a one-punch knockout loss at the hands of Marquez. Decision wins over Brandon Rios and Bradley were next on his ring ledger.

An entire generation of boxing writers can now spell "Pacquiao." Political commentators have learned the name too. In 2010, Manny was elected to the Filipino Congress as a representative from Sarangani province, One can argue that Vitali Klitschko (now mayor of Kiev and leader of the Ukrainian Democratic Alliance for Reform) is a genuine political leader whereas Pacquiao is not. But Manny is a powerful symbol and takes his responsibilities seriously. "Politics is different than sports," he says. "Politics is about the nation and the people. There is no way to compare politics to boxing."

On September 4, Tina arrived at the Liberty Theatre at 10:00 am and was brought to a room on the second floor where Pacquiao was seated with a small group of reporters in advance of the press conference.

Manny was casually dressed, wearing neatly pressed slacks and a sport jacket over a polo shirt. Tina took a seat five feet away from him. "To be this close to Manny again. I'm so excited," she said.

When the group interview ended, Tina and Manny were reintroduced and he was told that it was her seventy-fifth birthday.

"We met five years ago," Tina said. "I'm very happy that I get to see you again."

"I'm happy to see you too," Manny told her. "Happy birthday."

Several photographers took photographs of them together. Then everyone moved downstairs, and the press conference began.

Pacquiao is a 10-to-1 betting favorite over Algieri. He's the faster, stronger, more experienced fighter and hits harder. Chris has a good chin. But as Manny's trainer, Freddie Roach, notes, "It's great to have a good chin, but you can't rely on that. Good punchers outlast good chins."

Also, in Macau, Pacquiao will be the house fighter. The crowd can't fight. But the crowd (with its cheers, oohs, and aahs when the favorite lands) can influence the judges' perception of what they see in the ring.

That said; it's never easy at the elite level in boxing. Algieri showed his mettle when he came back from two first-round knockdowns to decision Ruslan Provodnikov (the only opponent to put him on the canvas) despite fighting the final eleven rounds with an eye that looked like something out of a Halloween horror movie.

There was a nice buzz in the Liberty Theatre. The press conference dragged on a bit too long (as they are wont to do). But it ended on an upbeat note with Pacquiao, speaking in Tagalog and giving "a hug to Filipinos all over the world."

Tina shook hands with Algieri and told him, "My heart is with Manny. But good luck to both of you."

"Thank you," Chris responded. Then he added, "If I was from the Philippines, my heart would be with Manny too."

It's a prizefight. Anything can happen.

"You know how Filipino people pray," Tina told me as we left the Liberty Theatre. "When Manny fights, we all pray for him. We will pray for him this time too."

Her face took on a pensive look.

"I hope the end is happy for Manny. Not the end of this fight, but the end when he is done with boxing. But this is life, so who knows."

Then Tina smiled.

"For a long time, I was not liking that I'm going to be seventy-five. And now, to see Manny again on my birthday, I love that today I'm seventy-five."

HBO's Delta Force reflects one of the ways in which the ever-expanding digital media is changing the presentation of boxing.

HBO's "Delta Force"

It's 2:00 pm on Thursday, July 24, 2014. Four men and a woman are in suite 2427 at The Affinia Hotel across the street from Madison Square Garden. Frank Villegas, James Pilott, Camile Maratchi, Albert Kim, and Matthew Chase are in the final stages of editing a half-dozen segments that will air on HBO's Saturday night telecast of Gennady Golovkin vs. Daniel Geale and Bryant Jennings vs. Mike Perez.

Twenty floors below, Cory Green sits in a room with an unmade bed. Green was up until four o'clock in the morning, editing video from the previous day's press conference into sixty-to-ninety-second segments for distribution to boxing fans via various digital platforms.

These people are at ground zero for a unit known internally at HBO as "The Delta Force."

"We understand that we're not Army Rangers," HBO Sports senior producer Dave Harmon says. "The name 'Delta Force' is meant to be ironic."

The goal of Delta Force is to bond with fans by capturing the pulse of fight week. The initiative had its origins in *24/7*, which was launched to coincide with the 2007 mega-fight between Oscar De La Hoya and Floyd Mayweather. *24/7* was premised on the belief that there are more stories to tell than the story of the fight itself and that telling these stories will strengthen the connections between HBO, individual fighters, and fans.

Face-Off, *2 Days*, *The Road To*, *Countdown*, and *Portrait of a Fighter* followed in the wake of *24/7*. All of these shows were created to engender interest in HBO Sports, increase viewership, and, ultimately, add to subscription buys. But there was room for improvement.

"We'd been doing features the same way for thirty years," Harmon recalls. "Go to the fighter's training camp. Shoot for a few days. But by creating our pre-produced features almost exclusively from that footage, we were locking ourselves in to what were sometimes old stories by the time they were on the air. And we almost always came up short where fight-week developments were concerned."

The Delta Force fills that hole in the creative process. It's a small agile production unit that can quickly shoot and edit high-quality video features. The first time it was utilized was for the 2010 pay-per-view bout between Manny Pacquiao and Joshua Clottey. In recent years, it has become crucial, not just to actual fight-night telecasts, but also to the marketing of HBO *World Championship Boxing* and *Boxing After Dark*, both of which have significantly smaller publicity budgets than HBO-PPV.

There was a time not long ago when viewers were encouraged to watch fights on television through advertising and articles in the print media. Now pipelines in the digital and social media universe connect content providers and consumers in remarkable ways.

Once a fight is announced, the Delta Force covers anything and everything: press conferences, gym workouts, weigh-ins, and the unexpected. It's in the field in the moment, capturing the reality of what's going on. Consumers—and in particular, young consumers—want "real time." Delta Force content is routinely packaged into shortform pieces and distributed to the public within twenty-four hours of shooting. At its best, it gives fans a deeper perspective on the fighters, the fight-week scene, and fight-related events.

The keys to the fulfillment of Delta Force's mission are production and distribution.

HBO Sports executive producer Rick Bernstein is the titular head of production. But the hands-on point person is vice president for creative development and operations Bill McCullough.

The first priority for production is having cameras in the right place at the right time. That takes planning, contacts, and luck. Some Delta Force content is spur-of-the-moment, go-with-the-flow footage. But most of it evolves from pre-planned storylines.

"It all starts with the schedule," McCullough says. "And we're always up against the clock. We want to be as timely as possible."

During fight week, a five-person Delta Force team arrives on-site between mid-Sunday and mid-Wednesday depending on the magnitude of the fight. The crew members are multi-talented. Each of them can shoot, edit, and do whatever else is called for to support the team in the moment.

The crew sets up a twenty-four-hour-a-day editing facility in a hotel room near the fight site. With today's technology, the ability to shoot and process original content is constantly being streamlined. The bulk of the editing is done on laptop computers. Most of the pieces are less than five-minutes long.

"The biggest challenge we face is time," says Villegas. "People don't understand how long it takes to cut and edit video."

"Sometimes you want to do more with a particular segment because the material is so interesting," Pilott notes. "But usually, we only have a minute or two, so we have to make hard choices."

Demographically, the pre-fight marketing material is designed to appeal to a young audience. Thus, most of the outlets on which it's disseminated are populated primarily by a young demographic.

The content is provided when, where, and how young people want it. YouTube is the primary distribution platform for Delta Force short-form pieces. Multiple HBO platforms (such as HBO.com and HBO's Facebook page) funnel viewers to the network's YouTube channel. The content is also distributed as "HBO Boxing News" to third-party media such as Yahoo, boxing websites, and various sports, entertainment, and news outlets, which sometimes embed the videos in online articles.

Fifty years ago, Marshall McLuhan wrote, "The medium is the message (i.e. the form of the medium by which a message is transmitted influences how the message is perceived)."

HBO's Delta Force embodies that philosophy.

Some thoughts on the light side of boxing.

Fistic Nuggets

Michael Buffer has the easiest job in the word. He puts on a tuxedo, gets in a boxing ring, says "let's get ready to rumble," announces a few fighters and some judges' scorecards, and makes thousands of dollars for each show. No pressure at all.

Right?

Wrong!

"I have this recurring anxiety dream," Buffer told me over lunch not long ago. "I've had it for years. There are variations on the theme, but it's basically the same dream. I have a show to do and I can't find my tuxedo; or I can't get out of my hotel room; or the car breaks down on the way to the arena; or I'm up in the top seats looking down and everyone at ringside is looking for me but I can't find my way down; or I'm at ringside, but I left my notes back at the hotel and I don't know who's fighting that night."

"I still have the dream every month or so that I'm aware of," Michael continued. "Now, if it wakes me up, I can laugh it off. The first few times, it wasn't funny."

Is the dream based on reality?

"Not really," Buffer answered. "I was nervous when I started ring announcing, but that was a long time ago. The closest real-life incident I've had that might relate to the dream was before a Mike Tyson fight in Atlantic City. I was on the elevator at Trump Plaza, wearing a tuxedo, going downstairs for the fight. A young woman looked at me and said, 'Your tie is crooked. Let me fix it for you.' I said okay, so she leaned forward and started adjusting my tie. Then the elevator door opened. And she literally tore the tie off me and ran away with it. I had to go to one of the restaurants and get a tie from a waiter so I could do my job that night."

★ ★ ★

In today's world of e-commerce, the prevailing currency is tweets and hits. With that in mind, writers for boxing websites are instructed to get Manny Pacquiao and Floyd Mayweather into as many headlines as possible. But why stop there?

According to Twitaholic.com, as of this writing, Katy Perry has 59,788,693 "followers." That's more than anyone else on the planet. Justin Bieber is in second place with 56,697,388. Barack Obama is third. President Obama, by the way, is credited with more than 12,000 "updates" since signing up for Twitter in 2007. One hopes than an aide rather than the president himself is doing all that tweeting.

Other tweeters with followings above the 25 million-mark include Taylor Swift (46,237,654), Lady Gaga (42,698,216), Britney Spears (39,515,790), Rihanna (37,879,423), Justin Timberlake (37,350,758), Ellen DeGeneris (34,029,235), Christiano Ronaldo (31,072,460), Jennifer Lopez (29,445,681), Shakira (27,604,808), and Oprah Winfrey (25,482,890).

LeBron James is the highest-ranked American sports figure with 16,101,870 followers. If LeBron could send out a tweet asking all of his followers to buy a copy of *The Final Recollections of Charles Dickens* (my new book), that would be really cool.

Among religious figures, the Dalai Lama checks in at 9,682,338.

Floyd Mayweather, Manny Pacquiao, and Mike Tyson are the three boxing personalities with the largest Twitter followings.

With that in mind, I'd suggest that an enterprising boxing website consider the following headlines for articles:

* Behind Closed Doors with Justin Bieber and Floyd Mayweather
* Did Lou DiBella Break Lady Gaga's Heart?
* What Rihanna and Chris Brown Could Learn from Mike Tyson
* Does Jennifer Lopez Have the Hots for Harold Lederman?
* Al Haymon to Co-Host Academy Awards with Ellen DeGeneris
* Separated at birth: Justin Timberlake and Bernard Hopkins
* Did Shannon Briggs Threaten to Punch Out Oprah?
* WBC to Honor Ronaldo with Interim World Cup Trophy
* Bob Arum Disses Britney Spears
* Taylor Swift and Joe Santoliquito to Wed
* Richard Schaefer to Sing Shakira's Biggest Hits
* Manny Pacquiao Voices Respect for the Dalai Lama

★ "Who the Fuck is Dolly Lama?" Floyd Mayweather Sr Asks
And one more for old times sake:
★ Is Don King Deader than Elvis?

* * *

Muhammad Ali was a guest in my homes many times. I've written
about some of those occasions, but I don't think I ever put the following
recollection on paper.

I make good hot fudge sauce. It's from an old Julia Child recipe.
Once, when Muhammad was at my home for dinner, I served hot fudge
sauce over vanilla ice cream for dessert. Muhammad's portion disappeared quickly. Then, in a show of appreciation—and with a twinkle in
his eye—he licked his bowl.

"That's great," I thought. "Muhammad likes my fudge sauce."

Then I had an epiphany on the unfairness of life.

"If Mike Tyson had done exactly the same thing, I'd be sitting here,
telling myself that Mike is disgusting and has no manners at all."

* * *

These are hard times for Don King. He still stops a room when he
enters. But his gait is slower than before, and he's no longer a controlling
force in boxing.

My most memorable moment with King came on October 29, 1984.
Don was fifty-two years old then and at the peak of his power.

I spent that day with Mike Jones, who managed WBC 140-pound
champion Billy Costello (one of King's fighters). Don and Mike were
engaged in a heated contract negotiation on the fourth floor of King's
East 69th Street townhouse in Manhattan.

The room looked like a Hollywood movie set. Thick red carpet,
leather sofas, a mirrored ceiling and fully mirrored wall, an enormous
desk and glass-topped conference table, three television sets, two huge
American flags.

Behind the desk, so they weren't visible from most parts of the room,
six television monitors that were linked to closed-circuit cameras allowed
King to monitor the rest of the townhouse.

King had a problem. Mike Jones wasn't bending to his will. Don sweet talked; he cajoled; he threatened. A Shakespearean rage was building. Finally, King picked the telephone off his desk and slammed it down. The receiver spun off and dangled in mid-air, twisting wildly. A stream of obscenities followed.

Then King stopped short, looked at me, and shouted, "That white motherfucker with the yellow pad is writing down everything I say."

★ ★ ★

This one is for aging boxing fans who suffer through ear-splitting rap music when they go to the fights.

Dmitriy Salita's Star of David Promotions recently hosted a night of club fights at Webster Hall in New York. One of the people in attendance was venerable publicist Bill Caplan, who grimaced through the music and recounted a night at the fights with his good friend Don Chargin.

Chargin promoted his first fight card at age twenty-three. Six decades later, he's still going strong. On August 25, 2012, Don promoted a night at the fights at The Sports Center in Fairfield, California. Earlier in the day, Caplan had given him a CD of Frank Sinatra's greatest hits. Knowing a good thing when he heard it, Chargin handed the CD to the arena DJ and told him, "This is what you play between fights tonight."

"What about the fighters' ringwalk music?"

"They can walk out to Sinatra," Chargin instructed. "If you play anything else, you're fired."

"None of the fighters or fans complained," Caplan recounts. "It was refreshing, to say the least."

★ ★ ★

Bob Arum has been known to lash out at adversaries. But part of the promoter's charm is that he says what he thinks about his own fighters too. That was on display at a March 11, 2014, press conference in New York.

Asked if he would advise Julio Cesar Chavez Jr with regard to which trainer he should hire, Arum answered, "Chavez is not the kind of guy you advise which trainer he should go to. You advise him to go to a trainer and hope you at least get that accomplished."

Then Arum came down hard on Mikey Garcia and Orlando Salido for failing to make weight for championship fights and opined, "This whole idea of fighters weighing in the day before a fight is insane. If they weighed in on the day of a fight, instead of dehydrating so much they'd fight at a higher weight class like they did in the old days when boxing was boxing."

That led to Arum being asked if he thought boxing should go back to fifteen-round championship contests.

"I was against the change to twelve rounds when it happened," the promoter acknowledged. "But I don't see any reason to go back to fifteen. Fifteen rounds might be less exciting because the fighters would be pacing themselves more."

Then Arum got a look in his eyes that signaled something good was coming.

"Besides," he added. "It's bad enough watching Guillermo Rigondeaux for twelve rounds. Who wants to watch fifteen?"

★ ★ ★

On Friday, April 11, 2014, a seventy-six-year-old man with a pleasant face sat at a round table in the media center at the MGM Grand in Las Vegas.

Duane Ford retired as an active boxing judge last year and is now president of the North American Boxing Federation. In a matter of hours, Manny Pacquiao and Tim Bradley would weigh-in for the rematch of their 2012 encounter. Oscar Valdez would be fighting Adrian Perez for the NABF super-featherweight title on the undercard. Hence Ford's presence.

Ford is one of two judges who ignited a firestorm of protest when he scored Pacquiao-Bradley I in favor of Bradley. Promoter Bob Arum led the assault. Now, looking around the media center, Duane recalled, "Things were pretty bad for a while. Everyone who owns a laptop is an expert on boxing. No judge would want to experience the brutal attacks I had to endure. My darkest day was having a United States senator [Harry Reid of Nevada] go on national television and say, 'My good friend, Duane Ford . . .'You know the rest."

"I have no regrets," Ford continued. "There were two rounds I gave to Bradley that were hard for me to call. I still think I got them right. But nothing that happens tomorrow night will mean I was right, and nothing that happens tomorrow night will mean I was wrong. That fight was two years ago."

As Ford was finishing those thoughts, Bob Arum came over to say hello. For much of the week, the promoter had been denigrating the upcoming bout between Floyd Mayweather and Marcos Maidana (promoted by rival Golden Boy Promotions) as "a 12-to-1 mismatch that no one wants to see because everyone already knows who will win."

"I hear they're bringing you back to judge Mayweather-Maidana," Arum said, putting a friendly hand on Duane's shoulder. "It's the only way they can sell it as a competitive fight."

★ ★ ★

Words of Wisdom from the Wives of Fighters

Terance Crawford's successful championship defense against Yuriorkis Gamboa in his hometown of Omaha has led to a revival of sorts for Ron Stander.

Stander was a club fighter from nearby Council Bluffs who challenged Joe Frazier in Omaha for the heavyweight crown in 1972. Frazier beat Stander down convincingly and knocked him out. The fight wasn't particularly memorable, but a quote from Stander's wife, Darlene, was. Before the bout, Mrs. Stander presciently noted, "You don't take a Volkswagen into the Indianapolis 500 unless you know a shortcut."

Then there's Vikki LaMotta, Jake LaMotta's child bride. A publisher named Donald Fine once offered Vikki a contract to write a book about her life. But Vikki's agent warned that Fine had a justified reputation for being difficult to deal with.

"I was married to Jake for ten years," Vikki responded. "How bad can Donald Fine be?"

Phyllis Wepner was married to Chuck Wepner in 1975 when "The Bayonne Bleeder" fought Muhammad Ali. We'll let Mr. Wepner, who was knocked out in the fifteenth round, tell that tale:

"I'd told everybody that, if I won, I was going to rent a bus, put all my friends in it, drive from here to California, pick up every female hitchhiker, and party for days and weeks and months. I loved to party, I had two ex-wives and a hundred girlfriends, and I was always known as a big party guy. A womanizer, my wives used to call me. If I'd been heavyweight champion of the world, I would have tried to take on the whole female population of the United States. But instead, what happened was, the day of the fight, I gave my wife a very sexy blue negligee. And I told her, 'I want you to wear this tonight, because after the fight you'll be sleeping with the heavyweight champion of the world.' When the fight was over, after I'd gotten stitched up, twenty-three stitches, I went back to the hotel. I was pretty much exhausted. My wife was in the room, waiting for me, wearing the negligee. And she said to me, 'Okay, bigshot. Do I go to the champ's room, or does he come to see me?'

★ ★ ★

From and about Promoters

David Greisman (on Roc Nation and 50 Cent): "Boxers who want to waste their money start rap labels. Rappers who want to waste their money start boxing promotional companies."

Gary Shaw (when asked to "be honest" regarding the difficulties in finalizing a deal for a "Super Six" fight between Andre Ward and Andre Dirrell): "I can't be honest. I'm a promoter."

Bob Arum: "Promoters talk all the time about competitive matchups. And most of the time, they're not telling the truth. They're just doing their job."

And one more from Bob Arum: "You've got Adrien Broner on the undercard of Mayweather-Maidana. Big fucking deal. What's he going to do? Tweet something with his genitals?"

★ ★ ★

If boxing's world sanctioning bodies ran the National Football League, we'd see the following playoff scenario:

★ The New York Jets would finish with a 3-and-13 record but be ranked #6 in the AFC in order to qualify for a playoff slot.

★ The Cincinnati Bengals would be paid step aside money so the Pittsburgh Steelers could take their place in the playoffs.

★ Ray Rice would be cleared to play because, in the words of one sanctioning body official, "Beating a lady is highly critical, but it is not a major sin or crime."

★ Each playoff game would have one "neutral" official. All of the other officials would be from the home state of one of the competing teams.

★ Sanctioning body officials would invade the players' locker rooms after the game and badger players for their game-worn jerseys.

★ Official replicas of the Lombardi Trophy awarded to the Super Bowl winner would be sold online at NFL.com.

And of course, there would be six Super Bowls, giving rise to a Super Bowl champion, a Silver Super Bowl champion, an Interim Super Bowl champion, a Diamond Super Bowl champion, a Super Bowl champion emeritus, and a Super Super Bowl champion."

★ ★ ★

Three Things You'll Never Read On A Boxing Website

Elvis Presley impersonator Gary Shaw thrilled the audience.

Kery Davis is the brains behind Al Haymon

Michael Buffer is changing his trademark phrase from "Let's get ready to rumble" to "Just fuckin' fight."

★ ★ ★

The most celebrated hair in the history of boxing belongs to Don King. Writers have waxed eloquent for decades about its propensity to rise toward the heavens and it being proof positive that King stuck his finger in a light socket while the current was flowing.

Among the younger set, Canelo Alvarez is known for the color of his hair. And fashion followers remember cornerman Danny Milano unceremoniously severing Paulie Malignaggi's hair extensions between rounds of a 2008 fight against Lovemore Ndou because they were interfering with Paulie's vision.

My own hair is a bit shaggy and on the long side. I've worn it that way for years. When I was young, I had a "Jewish Afro" (complemented for three weeks in 1976 with a Fu Manchu mustache). My hair is gray now and thinner than it once was. I still like it long. That might be out of style, but it's who I am.

All of which brings me to a really bad haircut I got earlier this year. The barber scalped me. Boxing people run the gamut from kind to diplomatic to blunt to cruel. So I went to the weigh-in for the next big fight at Madison Square Garden with a certain amount of trepidation.

David Diamante was the first person to comment on my hair. He said it looked "all right." But with all due respect, I don't need a guy who hasn't cut his dreadlocks since 1988 counseling me on my hair.

Then Michael Buffer had his say. When Michael talks about fashion and grooming, people listen.

"It makes you look younger," Buffer offered. "Do you remember when we were kids in the 1960s? You had all those old guys wearing their hair long, and all it did was make them look silly and older."

Michael was trying to be kind. It just didn't come out that way.

HBO's radiantly beautiful production coordinator Tami Cotel was next.

"It makes you look so handsome," Tami told me. "Your hair used to have a fuddy-duddy Albert Einstein look. All you need now is a little gel . . ."

Then Tami ran her fingers through my hair, showing me where the gel should be. I was starting to think, "This might not be so bad."

At which point, Tim Bradley walked by, took one look, and blurted out, "Oh, man! What did you do to your hair? It looks awful."

★ ★ ★

For those of you who wonder what the life of a boxing writer is like, here's a sampler.

Not long ago, I was reading *The Life and Adventures of Martin Chuzzlewit* by Charles Dickens when the telephone rang. There was no "Hi, Tom" or "This is Lou." The first words I heard were, "These motherfuckers better be careful or I'm going to blow them out of the water."

It was my good friend Lou DiBella, who is a man of passion and one of my favorite people in boxing. We talked for a while and then I went back to reading Dickens.

"It was a clear evening with a bright moon. The whole landscape was silvered by its light and by the frost, and everything looked exquisitely beautiful."

Ring ! ! !

I picked up the phone.

"Do you know what those motherfuckers just did?"

Agitated conversation. Then back to Dickens.

"I am in love with one of the most beautiful girls the sun ever shone upon. If I didn't tell her I loved her, where would be the use of my being in love?"

Ring ! ! !

"I can't stand it anymore. This is such a miserable fucking business."

"She is gone now. And of all unlikely things in this wide world, it is perhaps the most improbable that I shall ever look upon her face again."

Ring ! ! !

And so it went all afternoon. Dickens and DiBella. Two great men and some of the most memorable prose in the history of the English language.

★ ★ ★

And more on hair . . .

I was surprised earlier this year to see Lennox Lewis with a shaved head. Lennox had sported dreadlocks since 1995 and was proud of that look.

"What happened?" I asked.

"When I was boxing," Lennox told me, "I thought of my hair as a symbol of strength, like Samson. But that was then, and now is now. I'm more into business these days, so I'm showing the world a different look."

"I cut it off last year," Lennox continued. "I went to my barber in Miami and said, 'Do it.' There were no second thoughts, no regrets. You just haven't seen me since then."

"But I kept the hair," Lennox added. "It's hanging on the wall of my house in a frame that a friend designed for me. The way it looks now, it's a work of art."

★ ★ ★

A Few More Quotes

Kevin Rooney: "Who the hell knows what goes on in a fighter's mind in the ring? He may think he's getting laid when he punches a guy out."

Fight manager Bill Cayton (when told that Tommy Morrison, one of his fighters, was genuinely tough): "Unfortunately, he's also genuinely stupid."

Bernard Hopkins (at a pre-fight press conference for his second bout against Jean Pascal): "I'm going to beat him up in French too."

George Foreman (responding to the allegation that his victory over Michael Moorer was fixed): "Sure the fight was fixed. I fixed it with a right hand."

Issues and Answers

Floyd Mayweather is a superb fighter. He's also among the most polarizing figures in boxing.

Floyd Mayweather, Donald Sterling, and TMZ

Now that Floyd Mayweather vs. Marcos Maidana is over, boxing fans can refocus their attention on the story that the sports media has fixated on for the past ten days.

On April 25, 2014, TMZ posted a tape of a 9-minute-26-second telephone conversation between Los Angeles Clippers owner, eighty-year-old billionaire Donald Sterling, and a thirty-one-year-old woman named V. Stiviano. The conversation was recorded by Stiviano, who was once Sterling's mistress.

In the conversation, Sterling (who is battling prostate cancer) comes across as an unhappy old man. Stiviano appears to be leading, manipulating, and sometimes goading him into making racist comments. Sterling, after some initial resistance, obliges. The worst of Sterling's comments have been widely reported.

A firestorm of media coverage and protest followed the TMZ post. Barack Obama denounced Sterling's comments as "incredibly offensive." On April 29, NBA commissioner Adam Silver announced that Sterling had been fined $2,500,000 (the maximum fine that can be levied by the league under the circumstances) and banned for life from entering the team facilities or attending any team practice or NBA game. Silver further declared that, pursuant to the league constitution and by-laws, he would ask the other NBA owners to force Sterling to sell the team.

Stiviano now says that she "never meant to hurt" Sterling. That's a little like John Wilkes Booth saying that he never meant to hurt Abraham Lincoln. It wouldn't be surprising if her next step is to sell her story to the *National Enquirer* or pose for *Playboy*.

The media as a whole seems unconcerned with the fact that Sterling has humiliated his wife with public and private dalliances for years. It has also failed to fully explore numerous other issues.

If Sterling's remarks had been about Jews or gays, would the national uproar and punishment have been the same? Does anyone really think that Donald Sterling is the only NBA owner who harbors racist sentiments? What about Major League Baseball owners? The National Football League? Before the sports establishment gets a sore arm from patting itself on the back as a consequence of Sterling's punishment, let's reflect for a moment on the Washington Redskins, who are owned by Daniel Snyder.

Unlike "Blackhawks" and "Braves," Redskins is a derogatory term. Want proof? Use the term "Redskins" in a sentence that doesn't carry a negative connotation and is unrelated to the National Football League. Or phrased differently, what would happen if James Dolan suggested changing the name of the New York Knicks to the New York Colored People?

And what about Charles Barkley's comment on national television that the NBA is "a black league"? I love Charles Barkley as a commentator. But didn't he step over the line here? Suppose Barkley had called the NBA a "Christian league" or a "straight league"?

Perhaps the most thoughtful public commentary on the Sterling affair came from Kareem Abdul-Jabbar, who addressed it in an essay for *Time Magazine* with characteristic dignity and grace.

"The poor guy's girlfriend is on tape cajoling him into revealing his racism," Abdul-Jabbar wrote. "What a winding road she led him down to get all of that out. She blindfolded him and spun him around until he was just blathering all sorts of incoherent racist sound bites that had the news media peeing with glee."

"Racists," Abdul-Jabbar continued, "deserve to be paraded around the modern town square of the television screen so that the rest of us who believe in the American ideal of equality can be reminded that racism is a disease that we haven't yet licked. What bothers me about this whole Donald Sterling affair isn't just his racism. I'm bothered that everyone acts as if it's a huge surprise. [Sterling's racist conduct] has been going on for years, and this ridiculous conversation with his girlfriend is what puts you over the edge? That's the smoking gun? And shouldn't we be equally angered by the fact that his private intimate conversation was taped and then leaked to the media? The making and release of this tape is so sleazy that just listening to it makes me feel like an accomplice to the crime."

"Sterling," Abdul-Jabbar concluded, "is the villain of this story. But he's just another jerk with more money than brains."

That makes for a nice segue to Floyd Mayweather.

On April 29, Mayweather said of Donald Sterling, "I don't have nothing negative to say about the guy. He's always treated me with the utmost respect. He has always invited me to games, always. And he always says, 'Floyd, I want you to sit right next to me and my wife.'"

Malcolm X had a term for people of color who thought like that. And it wasn't pretty.

Then Mayweather inserted himself further into the Sterling dialogue by saying that he was interested in being part of a group that would buy the Clippers. But he cautioned, "I can't come in talking about Mayweather only gonna get three percent, four percent. I got to get a solid percentage. Do we want to buy the Clippers? Yes, we do. We are very very interested in buying the Clippers."

That's just the ownership the NBA needs after censuring Donald Sterling for racist comments.

Lest one forget; Mayweather was seen worldwide on UStream.com calling Manny Pacquiao a "little yellow chump," a "whore," and a "faggot." He also said, "Once I stomp the midget, I'll make that motherfucker make me a sushi roll and cook me some rice." For good measure, Floyd then added, "Motherfucker Pacquiao, he can't speak no English."

Closer to home insofar as the NBA is concerned, Mayweather reacted to the outpouring of media attention that Jeremy Lin received two years ago by tweeting, "All the hype is because he's Asian."

Mayweather owning an NBA franchise would also do wonders for the league's outreach to women.

Over the years, Floyd has had significant issues with women and the criminal justice system. In 2002, he pled guilty to two counts of domestic violence. In 2004, he was found guilty on two counts of misdemeanor battery for assaulting two women in a Las Vegas nightclub. In 2012, he served two months in prison after pleading guilty to charges relating to another indictment for domestic violence.

Nor are women likely to look fondly on Mayweather's recent decision to excoriate his former fiancée, Shantel Jackson, by informing the world via social media that she'd had an abortion and posting ultrasound images of "our twin babies" on his Facebook page and Instagram.

Mayweather, of course, had his own TMZ "Oops!" moment on March 12 of this year, when TMZ reported, "Floyd Mayweather allegedly orchestrated a savage attack on two of his employees he suspected of stealing his jewelry. Sources familiar with the situation tell TMZ Sports the two men had been hired to work on Floyd's Vegas homes. But when jewelry went missing, Floyd pointed the finger at them. We're told the men claim they were instructed to meet Floyd at an off-site location. When the men arrived, they claim Floyd was waiting for them—along with a number of his 'people' who proceeded to beat the living crap out of them with various weapons, including clubs. Our sources say the attack was so brutal the men could have easily died. Both men had broken arms and legs and were hospitalized for several days. We're told the men are adamant they never took anything from Floyd, and it appears Floyd realizes that now."

Two days later, TMZ posted a follow-up report that included X-rays purporting to show "a broken arm . . . a snapped pinkie . . . multiple fractures in the left hand that required pins to reset the bones . . . We're told the left arm was so badly broken, doctors drilled into the bone to attach a titanium plate so it would reset . . . Just a few of the injuries suffered by one of the men allegedly beaten by Floyd Mayweather's crew."

Here, it should be noted that TMZ's Mayweather report was undocumented beyond the unsourced allegations and anonymous X-rays. Unlike the matter of Donald Sterling, there was no tape of the beating. And unlike V. Stiviano, Mayweather's alleged victims chose to remain anonymous.

On March 24, Laura Meltzer (a public information officer for the Las Vegas Police Department) told the *New York Daily News*, "We've had a variety of reports that have come out stating this event occurred. We have not had a victim come forward to the police to make an official complaint. As of right now, the bureau commander is not aware of any complaint that has been officially filed. If this is a victim who is choosing not to come forward and make a report; then that's up to the victim. We don't have any say in that. There is no criminal complaint on file, so there is no reason to go and contact Mr. Mayweather."

That said; TMZ has a pretty good track record on reports of this nature. And there appears to be a culture of this sort of incident around

Mayweather. His Rolls Royce was spotted on the scene after an August 23, 2009, shooting outside a Las Vegas skating rink. One of his associates, Ocie Harris, was indicted on attempted murder charges for shooting at two passengers in another car, one of whom had reportedly insulted Mayweather. After the shooting, police searched Mayweather's house, looking for evidence, and seized handguns, ammunition, and bulletproof vests, none of which were used in the shooting. Harris's lawyer has said that his client was used as a pawn by police and prosecutors in an effort to link the shooting to Mayweather. Harris subsequently pled guilty to three felony charges and was sentenced to two to five years in prison.

Quite possibly, the TMZ report about the beating allegedly administered at Mayweather's command is unfounded. And Floyd is under no obligation to respond to every rumor about him that surfaces in the media. But the silence of Team Mayweather on the issue so far has been deafening.

It's also worth noting how little attention the story has received in the mainstream media. If this had been LeBron James or Peyton Manning, it would have been the lead story on ESPN SportsCenter and on the front or back page of every tabloid in America.

The fact that boxing's flagship fighter is at the center of these allegations is a problem. The fact that the mainstream media doesn't seem to care might be a bigger problem. It shows how little Mayweather (and boxing) now matter to the wider audience.

In 2015, Al Haymon became the dominant force in boxing. This article, written in July 2014, was a prelude to that.

What Is Al Haymon Planning?

Al Haymon is smart. "Scary smart," one person who has dealt with him over the years calls him. He's also adept at telling people what they want to hear, a good listener, and very much into control.

In recent months, Haymon has added significantly to the growing number of fighters that he manages or "advises." In a better-run sport, his recruiting methods might earn him a trip to the commissioner's office to answer charges of tampering. Be that as it may, the list of fighters that he represents now includes Floyd Mayweather, Marcos Maidana, Adrien Broner, Danny Garcia, Lucas Matthysse, Amir Khan, Devon Alexander, Deontay Wilder, Peter Quillin, Shawn Porter, Keith Thurman, Erislandy Lara, Paulie Malignaggi, Andre Berto, Chris Arreola, Sakio Bika, Gary Russell Jr, Adonis Stevenson, Chad Dawson, Beibut Shumenov, Jermain Taylor, Edwin Rodriguez, Lamont and Anthony Peterson, Jermell and Jermall Charlo, Leo Santa Cruz, John Molina, Rances Barthelemy, Luis Collazo, Josesito Lopez, Miguel Vasquez, Vanes Martirosyan, Dominic Breazeale, Marcus Browne, Terrell Gausha, Errol Spence Jr, Dominic Wade, and Rau'shee Warren.

That's a lot of fighters. And it leads to the question: "What will Haymon do with them?" Showtime, which supplanted HBO as his primary purchaser of content, doesn't have the budget for license fees to keep them all active.

The boxing industry has been kept largely in the dark with regard to Haymon's plans for the future. Over the past few weeks, this writer has conducted dozens of interviews in an effort to put the puzzle pieces together. An outline is emerging.

Let's start with some basics.

Haymon signs fighters to an "Exclusive Advisory Agreement" that gives his corporation the exclusive right to render services in securing the boxer's participation in professional boxing matches, exhibitions, entertainment performances, personal appearances, endorsements, and sponsorship opportunities that arise out of the fighter's boxing career.

In return, Haymon is required to (a) use his "best efforts" to secure remunerative boxing matches for the boxer; (b) advise and counsel the boxer in the overall development of his career; (c) secure proper training facilities and equipment for the boxer; (d) publicize and promote the talents and abilities of the boxer in the media; and (e) attempt to secure commercial endorsements, personal appearances, and entertainment opportunities for the boxer.

Haymon often charges 10 or 15 percent of a fighter's purse for his services. That's less than the standard manager's share. Sometimes, he'll pay an advance to a fighter and only cut the fighter's purse after the purse reaches a certain level. The advance is paid back only when the purses reach a still-higher number.

Haymon isn't Mother Teresa. He makes money from boxing, and not just from his managerial share.

For example, Haymon has had the contractual right to buy millions of dollars worth of tickets at face value for certain Floyd Mayweather fights. One promoter recounted being in Las Vegas for Oscar De La Hoya vs. Mayweather, having two prime tickets, and needing three. So he traded his two tickets to Haymon in exchange for three less desirable ones. An hour later, those two tickets were listed on the Internet for $12,000.

Haymon's relationship with Lamon Brewster raises a more complicated set of issues.

Sam Simon was one of the co-creators of *The Simpsons* and an avid sports fan. In 1999, he became Brewster's manager. "Boxing isn't a source of revenue for me," Simon said at the time. "But I take my responsibilities very seriously and get very involved emotionally in Lamon's fights."

On April 10, 2004, Brewster knocked out Wladimir Klitschko to become WBO heavyweight champion. Then Haymon came calling.

"Haymon wasn't the power in boxing then that he would become," Simon recalled several years ago. "But his modus operandi was pretty much the same. He sought Lamon out and told him, 'Hey, brother. You look like you could use some good representation from someone who cares about you.'" Before long, Simon was out and Haymon was

Brewster's advisor. Thereafter, Lamon suffered a detached retina in his left eye in the first round of an unsuccessful April 1, 2006, title defense against Sergei Liakhovich. But that doesn't tell the whole story. Yes, Brewster suffered a detached retina during the fight. But his eye was injured before the bout. He'd undergone laser eye surgery several weeks prior to the fight. A review of Ohio State Athletic Commission records reveals that this history was covered up during the pre-fight paperwork and examination process.

Worse; one year later, Brewster went to Germany under Haymon's watch for a rematch against Klitschko while he was still on medical suspension in the United States. Two of Lamon's sparring partners told Keith Idec of the *New Jersey Herald News* that, prior to fighting Klitschko, Brewster was having difficulty seeing out of his left eye. Lamon lost every minute of the Klitschko rematch, which was stopped after six rounds.

Brewster ended his career as a human punching bag for the likes of Gbenga Okoukon and Robert Helenius. He is now vision-impaired and, possibly, legally blind in one eye.

Haymon is now boxing's most influential power broker. The cornerstone of his empire was a relationship that evolved with HBO and, in particular, with Kery Davis (the network's point person on boxing from the turn of the millennium until June 2013).

Haymon got dates for his fighters on HBO. And as long as he could control the promotion, he didn't seem to care much who the promoter of record was.

In the boxing business, a person can be black or white, American or foreign-born, straight or gay, and survive. The one thing he cannot be is weak. Haymon smells out weakness and exploits it well. He maneuvered promoters into putting his fighters on their cards for a fraction of their normal promotional percentage and without the fighter being signed to the promoter. Some promoters bellowed like harpooned seals that they weren't getting their fair share of the pie. But they stood in line for their cut of the television license fees that Haymon doled out to them.

Haymon has a lot of people's testicles in his pocket. Greg Bishop found that out in 2011, when he began researching a profile on Haymon for the *New York Times*. Dozens of people whom Bishop called either declined comment or failed to return his telephone calls. An attorney for

Haymon sent a cease-and-desist letter to the *Times*. To Bishop's dismay, his article was substantially toned down before publication at the instruction of his editor.

Meanwhile, Haymon has an aversion to being interviewed by the media and operates largely out of public view. One might posit that there are people in the federal witness protection program who get more exposure than he does.

A manager who was angry that Haymon was attempting to sign one of his fighters recently hired an investigator to search public records and compile information on Haymon. The only thing of note in the report was the suggestion that, at various times, Haymon has used the alias "Brian K. Pitts."

So . . . what should boxing expect next from Haymon?

Earlier this year, Haymon formed a new company, a Nevada-based LLC called Haymon Sports. The company has rented office space (suite 350 at 3930 Howard Hughes Parkway in Las Vegas).

Haymon initially planned to use Golden Boy as the primary promotional vehicle for his fighters during the next stage of his journey through boxing. Toward that end, he appears to have coordinated with former Golden Boy CEO Richard Schaefer in an effort to buy out Oscar De La Hoya and the company's other major shareholders (AEG and the Brener family). That plan hit a roadblock when De La Hoya refused to sell."

"I'm the Golden Boy, not Richard Schaefer," Oscar said. "It's my name and it's my company."

After buy-out negotiations failed, Schaefer resigned from Golden Boy. On June 16, 2014, the company instituted an arbitration proceeding against him, claiming $50,000,000 in damages.

At the same time, Haymon was trying to raise money (at least $100,000,000) to underwrite a new venture. Creative Artists Agency (one of the top talent and sports agencies in the world) was approached but chose not to become involved in the fundraising process. Ultimately, Haymon settled on CVC Capital Partners and Waddell & Reed (both of whom are among the primary equity owners of the Formula One Group). Bruce Hardy McClain (a former managing partner of CVC and currently a member of the CVC board of directors) is also on the board of directors of Haymon Sports.

As noted earlier, Haymon already has more fighters than Showtime has dates for. And his stable of fighters keeps growing. Thus, to get to the next stage, he has approached many of the major sports channels about televising his fighters.

The NBC Sports Group expressed interest.

Multiple sources say that NBC has agreed in principle to a plan pursuant to which Haymon's company (or a stand-in) would buy $20,000,000 worth of time on NBC and televise at least twenty fights cards during a one-year period. Most of the fights would be on the NBC Sports channel, but at least three would be on NBC.

Haymon's investment group would pay most costs associated with the telecasts, including the fighters' purses and television production costs. It would hope to recoup these costs through the sale of advertising. The plan is sufficiently far along that one talent agency has begun putting together a list of names that it can offer as television commentators.

And after the first year?

Sources say that Haymon is considering transitioning to an online subscription service that would bypass television networks and PPV carriers by dealing directly with consumers. Toward that end, he has hired Alex Balfour (who was head of new media for the London Olympic Committee). Balfour is believed to be soliciting applications from potential employees who would like to work for the subscription venture. Balfour's website (www.alexbalfour.com) says that he is "currently the Chief Digital Officer of a new, exciting, start up in sport."

The above plan is similar to a twenty-four-hour-a-day subscription Internet channel that World Wrestling Entertainment launched earlier this year. The cost to subscribers for the WWE channel is $9.95 per month. But subscriptions have fallen far short of expectations and, because of operation and programming costs, WWE is expected to lose at least $40,000,000 during the coming year. That poor performance is a major reason why WWE stock has dropped by more than 60 percent (a loss in market value in excess of one billion dollars) since March of this year.

But launching a subscription channel might not be Haymon's ultimate goal. His endgame after that could be taking the company public pursuant to a plan whereby he and the initial investors would reap significant gains through a public stock offering. But—and this is a big but—going public means a different standard of disclosure and more stringent ethical requirements for the conduct of business.

Whatever the plan, one thing is clear. Haymon isn't doing this as a charitable venture. A significant portion of the investors' money that will be spent in the near future is likely to be spent on content (i.e., fight cards provided by Haymon).

The investors might do well. Or the investors might lose a lot of money.

Haymon did not respond to requests for an interview in conjunction with this article. Stephen Espinoza (the head of Showtime Sports) declined through an intermediary to answer questions. Richard Schaefer responded by telephone and said that, due to the pendency of litigation, he would prefer not to discuss the situation publicly at the present time.

That leaves a lot of unanswered questions such as, "What will Floyd Mayweather's role be in all of this?"

Then there's the matter of litigation.

On June 16, 2014, Bad Dog Productions filed a lawsuit against Haymon and several other defendants in state court in Florida. The lawsuit alleges tortious interference with contract and other claims in conjunction with super-featherweight Rances Barthelemy (who signed with Haymon earlier this year). Similar claims by other promoters and managers who believe that Haymon acted improperly to their detriment might follow. Many of these lawsuits will have little more than nuisance value. But one piece of litigation has the potential to become a major problem.

On April 29, 2014, Main Events filed suit in the United States District Court for the Southern District of New York against Haymon, Golden Boy, Showtime, Adonis Stevenson, Yvon Michel, and Groupe Yvon Michel (Michel's promotional company). The suit alleges multiple causes of action against the defendants, including claims of tortious interference with contract and interference with prospective economic advantage against Haymon in conjunction with the falling apart of the proposed light-heavyweight title-unification bout between Sergey Kovalev (promoted by Main Events) and Adonis Stevenson (now managed by Haymon).

Main Events is represented in the litigation by Pat English. There's a school of thought that there are two people in the boxing industry that one doesn't want to have as an angry adversary. One is James Prince. The other is English.

It's impossible to know at the present time how the Main Events litigation will play out. It's possible that plaintiff will drop its claims against Golden Boy in exchange for the promotional company providing evidence against Haymon. English himself has said, "We filed the lawsuit based on the facts that we know with certainty at the present time. As we take discovery and the case unfolds, it's possible, if not likely, that additional causes of action against Haymon will be added in an amended complaint."

There's also the matter of the arbitration proceeding between Golden Boy and Richard Schaefer.

When Schaefer resigned as Golden Boy CEO on June 2, he issued a statement that read, "After more than ten years with Golden Boy, it is time to move on to the next chapter of my career. This decision has required a great deal of personal reflection, but ultimately I concluded that I have no choice but to leave. I have succeeded in banking and I have succeeded in boxing, and I look forward to the next opportunity. I am proud to remain a shareholder, so I have a strong interest in the continued success of the company. I am proud of what we have accomplished at Golden Boy, but I now look forward to new challenges."

On June 13, Golden Boy chief operating officer Bruce Binkow (who was widely regarded as Schaefer's righthand man) left Golden Boy. Then, on June 30, De La Hoya fired deputy COO Armando Gaytan, executive vice president Raul Jaimes, and vice president of marketing Nicole Sparks. Jaimes's aunt is married to Schaefer. Gaytan is married to Nicole Becerra (Schaefer's longtime executive assistant, who left the company shortly after Schaefer's departure). Sparks reported to Binkow.

Meanwhile, Schaefer's relationship with Haymon is at the heart of Golden Boy's claim against its former CEO. Schaefer can be expected to argue in the arbitration proceeding that (1) whatever he did with Haymon was designed to benefit Golden Boy; (2) De La Hoya was an impediment to Golden Boy functioning properly; (3) he offered to buy Oscar and the other shareholders out at a fair price; (4) when it was clear that the friction between himself and De La Hoya was hurting the company, he resigned; and (5) Golden Boy appears willing to continue doing business with Haymon without having "paper" on all of Haymon's fighters, which is no different from the practice that Schaefer himself followed.

Be that as it may; the arbitration proceeding (like the Main Events litigation) has the potential to uncover facts that are damaging to Haymon. And some of those facts might substantiate the claim that Haymon has achieved his present position in boxing through improper conduct encompassing both technical violations and more substantial violations of law.

For example, the Muhammad Ali Boxing Reform Act creates a firewall between managers and promoters. A manager is defined as "a person who receives compensation for service as an agent or representative of a boxer." A promoter is defined as "the person primarily responsible for organizing, promoting, and producing a professional boxing match." The act makes it "unlawful for a manager (i) to have a direct or indirect financial interest in the promotion of a boxer; or (iii) to be employed or receive compensation or other benefits from a promoter, except for amounts received as consideration under the manager's contract with the boxer."

Haymon purports to be a manager. But he functions as the de facto promoter for many of the shows on which his fighters appear. Often, he negotiates the license fee with the television network, selects many of the fighters who appear on the card, determines the purse for one or more of the fighters, and tells the promoter of record how much the promoter will be paid.

Most of Haymon's contracts with fighters state that they are governed by California law. But it appears that few if any of the contracts were signed before a representative of the California State Athletic Commission or filed with the commission as required by California law.

Haymon is also licensed as a manager in Nevada. But few if any of his contacts have been filed with the Nevada State Athletic Commission.

Contract filings in New York are a sloppy murky area of the law. Haymon's boxer-manager contracts might not be recognized by the New York State Athletic Commission because they're not on New York's standard form. But because they're not on the New York form, they also might not have to be filed with the NYSAC.

The wild card in all of this is that discovery in one or more of the aforementioned legal proceedings might lead to revelations that encourage law enforcement authorities to become involved. No one expects the United States Department of Justice to enforce the Ali Act. It would be nice if it did, but it hasn't so far. That's unlikely to change anytime soon. Nor are state authorities likely to enforce contract-filing requirements in a meaningful way.

But there's a time-honored axiom in law enforcement: "Follow the money."

If someone were to track what happened to the total license fees paid for each of the televised shows that Al Haymon's fighters have been involved with, things might get interesting. For example, shifting license fees from one fight to another is improper when it has the effect of disadvantaging a particular fighter, manager, or promoter without that person's knowledge. Here, one might note that, under federal law, certain revenue streams paid to promoters must be accurately disclosed to fighters.

There has been a lot of talk lately about Al Haymon being on the verge of "taking over boxing." Under the Al Haymon model, it has been said, Haymon would control everything within his universe (including all sources of revenue) the way UFC does in the world of mixed martial arts.

But if the past fifty years are any guide, it's impossible for one entity or person to control boxing. Don King was going to take over boxing. Bob Arum was going to take over boxing. Josephine Abercrombie and *The Contender* were going to take over boxing. It doesn't happen. Haymon could make a lot of money and amass even more power than he currently has. Or the weight of the boxing world could come crashing down on his investors and his own head.

As for the near future, perhaps the Haymon fighters who are signed to promotional contracts with Golden Boy will appear on Showtime, while his other fighters will be on NBC. Maybe the inverse will hold true. Golden Boy seems to be holding out hope that it can arrive at an understanding with Haymon that will allow it to continue promoting at least some of his elite fighters. If that doesn't happen, it's possible that Golden Boy will sue Haymon for various economic torts. If Richard Schaefer can free himself of the restrictions inherent in his contract with Golden Boy—restrictions that are said to run until 2018—he might be the ideal co-strategist and promoter of record for Haymon to work with.

As for Haymon's fighters; unlike a promoter (who has only an obligation of fair dealing), a manager has a fiduciary duty to his fighters. Right now, Haymon's fighters are corporate assets. And since they're already signed, there's little liability attached to them given the fact that Haymon hasn't promised them much more on paper than his advice, counsel, and "best efforts" to perform certain tasks on their behalf.

Has Haymon told his fighters what he plans to do with their con-. tracts as a corporate asset? Should he be making full disclosure of his future plans to them?

No sport other than boxing would allow itself to be in this situation. In any other sport, if one or more major players were planning an initiative that had the potential to restructure or fundamentally change the balance of power in the industry, it would be the subject of in-depth inquiry and investigation. But boxing has no sense of collective good. Virtually everything that happens in the sweet science today is dictated by the desire to curry favor with the powerful, the fear of reprisal, and selfish shortsighted economic interest.

*Like much of what goes on in boxing, the implementation of instant video
review is easer said than dome.*

Instant Video Review and Boxing

The November 8, 2014, title unification bout between Bernard
Hopkins and Sergey Kovalev was notable for several reasons, including
the fact that it marked the readiness to use instant video review on one
of boxing's biggest stages.

Referees are sometimes called upon to make judgment calls when
they're not in position to clearly see what happened. Watching fights
becomes a more satisfying experience and it's in the best interest of boxing if officials get critical calls right. Instant video review has worked well
in sports like football, baseball, basketball, and tennis. So one would think
it's a given that instant video review should be used in boxing.

But it's not that simple.

There's ample precedent for a commission overturning a referee's
call on the basis of video evidence after a fight has ended.

The California State Athletic Commission employed video review
at a hearing after the 2011 fight between Bernard Hopkins and Chad
Dawson. Hopkins claimed that a fight-ending shoulder injury had
resulted from his being illegally body-slammed to the canvas. Referee
Pat Russell saw things differently and awarded a second-round knockout
to Dawson. The CSAC changed the result to "no contest."

The New York State Athletic Commission used video replay after the
fact to overturn the verdict in a 2007 fight between Terrance Cauthen
and Raul Frank. Cauthen was leading on all scorecards when he was
accidentally head-butted on the chin and knocked woozy. Referee
Ricky Gonzalez didn't see the headbutt, stopped the fight, and declared
Frank the winner by knockout. After a hearing, the result was changed
to "no contest."

The NYSAC also used video review for a 2007 fight between
Delvin Rodriguez and Keenan Collins. The bout was originally ruled
"no contest" after Collins suffered a fight-ending cut above his left eye

that referee Eddie Claudio ruled was caused by an accidental clash of heads. A review of the tape at a later date showed that the cut was caused by a punch. The result was changed to a second-round knockout in Rodriguez's favor.

Nevada allows for video review, but only at the referee's request and only in instances where a fight-ending injury or knockout has occurred. In other words, the referee himself has to say, "I'd like to look at the video." Then the referee himself decides if he made the correct call. There's a TV monitor at ringside reserved for the use of video replay. Because the fight has ended, there's ample time for review. The procedure has been utilized in Nevada for MMA on several occasions but has yet to be employed for boxing.

Mohegan Sun also uses video review in fight-ending situations. There, the commission (not the referee) decides whether or not to use it and rules on the result. The aforementioned Delvin Rodriguez was the beneficiary of a ruling based on video review in conjunction with his 2013 bout against Freddy Hernandez. The fight was stopped after Hernandez was cut above the left eye. Referee Harvey Dock mistakenly ruled that the cut was caused by an accidental clash of heads, and Rodriguez was awarded a technical decision based on the judges' scorecards at that time. After review, the decision was changed to a knockout.

The Pennsylvania State Athletic Commission, if requested to do so by a fighter's camp, will hold a post-fight hearing to review video evidence in conjunction with a ruling on any accidental or intentional foul.

November 8 in New Jersey was a different from the above situations. The New Jersey State Athletic Control Board was prepared to use *instant* video review during a boxing match for the first time.

The first prerequisite for any instant video review procedure in boxing is that it cannot interfere with the flow of the fight. In other sports, officials can stop the flow of the action. That can't be done in boxing.

"This isn't football," Greg Sirb (executive director of the Pennsylvania State Athletic Commission and former president of the Association of Boxing Commissions) observes. "There's a one-minute rest period between rounds. Other than the time allotted for recovery from a low blow, that's it. The replay cannot be the equivalent of a time out for a fighter."

Within that framework, instant video review can be particularly useful in instances where officials are trying to determine whether a cut was caused by a punch or a head butt. That's because, in theory, that particular call isn't time sensitive. A cut fighter is supposed to fight until a ring doctor determines that he's no longer able to continue. Only then is it essential to rule with finality on the cause of the cut.

Additionally, instant review could be useful in determining whether a punch was thrown before or after the bell ending a round.

It has been suggested that instant video review also be employed to determine whether a knockdown should or shouldn't have been called in a particular instance. That's more problematic unless the determination is made before the judges turn in their scores for the round in question. It's easy to change 10-8 for Fighter A to 10-9 for Fighter A if a knockdown is taken away. But maybe, without the knockdown, a judge would have scored the round 10-10 or 10-9 for Fighter B.

And yes, officials can be told to mark various contingency scores on their scorecard for use in the event that a knockdown ruling is overturned. But given the limitations of some judges, that's a recipe for disaster.

In most instances, whether or not to deduct a point for a low blow or pushing an opponent's head down is a cumulative call that results from multiple misdeeds, not just one infraction.

As for whether a ten-count was too fast; officials can't re-do the end of a fight.

Was the count too slow? It's not practical to stop a fight and tell a fighter, "Sorry; we checked the tape and you were knocked out two minutes ago."

"We'll have to play some of these issues by ear," Larry Hazzard (director of the New Jersey State Athletic Control Board) acknowledged several days before Hopkins-Kovalev. "If a situation occurs where either the commission or a fighter's chief second requests a video review, we'll do it. All other sports have made an effort to correct human error by officials. For some reason, boxing has been reluctant to come out of the dark ages. The time to do it is now."

On November 8, HBO (which was televising Hopkins-Kovalev) installed a monitor at the commission table. Hazzard had a headset that enabled him to watch and hear what viewers saw at home. He did not have the ability to "call up" multiple camera angles from the production truck or view replays multiple times.

That highlights one of the problems inherent in utilizing instant video review in boxing.

Under the National Football League's replay system, four people (designated under NFL Rules as a technician, replay assistant, video operator, and communicator) advise and assist the referee on video reviews. The referee can watch a replay as many times and from as many camera angles as he wants before making a final call.

By contrast, few, if any, state athletic commissions have the funds and technological expertise necessary to implement even the most basic instant video review. That means, for the foreseeable future, it will only come into being if television provides the technology and financial resources. The network televising a fight could install a recording device at the commission table that allows a review official to cue up video segments as many times as desired. But that would require more technological expertise and cost more money.

Thus, instant video review might work well for fights with big-budget television coverage. But if boxing gets to a place where there's one set of rules for fights on major television networks and a different set of rules for everyone else, then boxing is in the wrong place.

There's also a potential problem in that television networks sometimes have an institutional interest in the outcome of a fight. Suppose the network has a camera-angle video that could lead to overturning a referee's call. But for whatever reason, in the heat of the moment, it isn't shown to home viewers or, under a more advanced system, put on a special commission video monitor. Either the people in the truck didn't realize its importance or there was a technological glitch. The network could be dragged into an ugly controversy.

Over the years, I've talked with numerous fighters about the possibility of instant video review. In most instances, their response has been that it's nice to get the calls right, but boxing needs competent unbiased referees more than it needs instant video review.

Fighters feel that a missed call is often the result of bias on the part of the referee rather than human error. And they believe that this bias is reflected, not just in isolated missed calls, but in the flow of the entire fight.

Fighters also believe that the state athletic commission officials who appoint biased referees do so with an awareness of their bias in the same way that they appoint judges with knowledge of their bias (for example, Gale Van Hoy in Texas). One can argue that instant video review would correct these biases. But many fighters believe that decisions regarding when the commission calls for a video review and how it interprets the video would simply give commission officials another tool to tilt the playing field further in favor of the house fighter.

These same fighters like the idea of a back-up referee at ringside who the referee can consult with if he's uncertain about a particular call. The back-up referee would also have the responsibility of communicating with the referee if he thinks a call was wrong.

"Are you sure?" would mean that the back-up referee saw things differently. If the primary referee had doubts about his call, he could make a correction. Consultations like this occur in football and basketball all the time without the use of video review.

As for November 8 in New Jersey, there were no controversial rulings by referee David Fields in Hopkins-Kovalev or Harvey Dock in Sadam Ali vs. Luis Carlos Abregu (the opening televised fight of the evening) that required instant video review. But give Hazzard credit for taking the first steps to put a review system in place.

"We have to start somewhere," Hazzard says. "Half a loaf is better than none. There's always some fear when you go into the unknown. But I think that video review will make things fairer for the fighters by correcting mistakes, and it's necessary to bring boxing in line with twenty-first-century sports. So let's make it work."

As a contrast to "Fistic Nuggets," these "Notes" were on the serious side.

Fistic Notes

A significant date passed largely unnoticed earlier this year. February 6, 2014, marked the tenth anniversary of Lennox Lewis's retirement from boxing.

On June 8, 2002, Lewis knocked out Mike Tyson in Memphis to solidify his status as the best heavyweight in boxing. His only bout after that was a June 6, 2003, battle against Vitali Klitschko in which Lennox struggled early before stopping Klitschko on cuts.

Fast forward to January 2004. It was a bitter cold day in New York. Lennox asked if I'd meet with him at an office he maintained in midtown. When I got there, he posed the question, "If I retire now without fighting a rematch against Klitschko, do you think it will hurt my legacy?"

"No," I answered. "Five years from now, people will look at your record and all they'll see next to Vitali's name is 'KO 6.' If you never fight again, you'll go down in history as the dominant heavyweight of your time and the man who broke the American stranglehold on the heavyweight title. You'll also be one of only three heavyweight champions who retired while still champion and stayed retired."

"I know Rocky Marciano was one," Lennox responded. "Who was the other?"

"Gene Tunney."

"Tunney was white, wasn't he?"

"Yes."

There was a pause for reflection.

"All right," Lennox said. "Will you write a retirement speech for me?"

We talked for a while about the thoughts that Lennox wanted to express. Among the things he said the following month in announcing his retirement were:

★ "Deciding to end my career as a professional boxer was not an easy decision to make. In many ways, continuing to fight would be the easiest course of action. I've been offered millions of dollars to fight again, which is all the more tempting because I believe that there are more championship-quality fights in me."

★ "Being heavyweight champion is a role that carries with it responsibilities that go far beyond the ring. As a competitor, as a professional, and as a human being, I have tried to do my best to fulfill these responsibilities. I've tried to treat people with respect. I've tried to demonstrate the importance of hard work and sacrifice in achieving goals. I have lived by the code that, if a job is worth doing, it should be done properly."

★ "A special thank you to each of the men I've fought. They are part of my story and their names will go down in history in the record book next to mine."

★ "Emanuel Steward did as much for me as any trainer ever did for a boxer. There were times when Manny believed in me more than I believed in myself."

★ "I am proud that I have the luxury of ending my career on my own terms."

Lennox is forty-eight years old now. During the past decade, he has resisted offers of tens of millions of dollars to come out of retirement. He has maintained his dignity and will always be a champion.

★ ★ ★

Seanie Monaghan sat in seat 28D on Delta Airlines flight 406, readying to fly from New York to Las Vegas. It was 10:37 am on Tuesday, April 8, 2014. The plane was filled to capacity with passengers traveling to Sin City to gamble. Seanie would be taking a bigger gamble than any of them. On Saturday night, he'd enter a boxing ring at the MGM Grand Garden Arena to do battle in the opening bout on the Pacquiao-Bradley 2 undercard.

Unlike his fellow passengers, Seanie would be punched in the face multiple times before the week was done. If someone on flight 406 returned to New York missing a tooth or with stitches above his eye, Seanie was likely to be the one. But he was also more likely than his fellow passengers to come home a winner.

Seanie isn't a celebrity fighter. Heads didn't turn when he boarded the plane. He looked like just another guy going to Las Vegas. But if there were a disruptive passenger, Seanie is the one the flight crew would be happy to have onboard to help subdue him.

The plane left the gate on schedule. Then the pilot came on the loudspeaker system.

"Right now, we're number ten for take-off. Things are moving slowly this morning because of the fog."

There was a collective groan from the passengers.

"I don't mind it," Seanie said. "When I fought in Vegas last year, my wife and Sammy (their two-year-old son) came with me. Now we have a daughter, Malia, who's five weeks old. She's too young to travel. As great as it is to have children, this is quiet time for me."

After a delay of twenty minutes, the plane took off.

"Vegas is okay for a few days," Seanie noted. "I'll be pretty much holed up in my room trying to make weight. Right now, making weight is more on my mind than the fight. I woke up this morning at 182. I have to make 175 by Friday. It won't be a problem, but I'm looking forward to being able to eat like a human being again."

The WBC Continental Americas championship belt was lodged in the bin overhead.

"I didn't check it because I was afraid I'd never see it again," Seanie said. "I've had it for about a year-and-a half-now. That would be a hell of a way to lose it."

Seanie's opponent in Las Vegas on Saturday night would be Joe McCreedy.

"I'm 20 and 0. His record is something like 15-and-6. It's no big deal if he loses to a guy who's 20 and 0. But if I lose to a guy who's 15 and 6, my career nosedives. There's pressure on me because of that. But at least I'll be able to sleep through the night this week. My wife has the hard job now."

Note: Monaghan broke McCreedy down with body shots. Referee Jay Nady stopped the bout after the third knockdown at 2:25 of round five.

★ ★ ★

The never-ending exploration of Mike Tyson's psyche continued earlier this year with a fine article by Don McRae in *The Guardian*. One passage offers a clue regarding Tyson's physicality with women and is particularly revealing.

Tyson told McRae, "Once, my mother was fighting with this guy, Eddie. And it's barbaric. Eddie knocked out her gold tooth, and me and Denise [Tyson's sister] are screaming. But my mother's real slick. She puts on a pot of boiling water. The next thing I know, she's pouring boiling water over Eddie. He was screaming, his back and face covered in blisters. So you see, I used to look upon women as being equal in a physical confrontation. I remember my mother—boom! boom!—attacking these men. I would take women very seriously. If you sleep, they might kill you."

★ ★ ★

The May 3, 2014, encounter between Floyd Mayweather and Marcos Maidana was a much better fight than it was expected to be. Floyd is still technically brilliant. He still knows all the tricks. Against Maidana, he sat down more on his punches than in the past and showed a fighting heart.

But at age thirty-seven, Mayweather is losing his legs. That was evident early in the fight. And his box office appeal may be dwindling.

Floyd is a big draw, but he has always needed a dance partner to generate stratospheric numbers. He was only half of the equation for the dollars that flowed from fights against Oscar De La Hoya and Canelo Alvarez. Best estimates are that Mayweather-Maidana (like Mayweather vs. Robert Guerrero) engendered under 900,000 pay-per-view buys. That means Showtime could lose millions of dollars on the event. And one day before Mayweather-Maidana, thousands of tickets were selling on secondary market sites such as TiqIQ.com for as much as 45 percent off list price.

Want more on where Mayweather ranks in contemporary culture?

Two days before Mayweather-Maidana, a Google search for "Floyd Mayweather" brought up 4,310,000 "results." That's an impressive number. But that same day, a Google search for *Game of Thrones* brought up 548,000,000 results. In other words, interest in Mayweather ran at less than eight-tenths of 1 percent of the interest in *Game of Thrones*.

★ ★ ★

Like Cary Grant clinging to the edge of a cliff in *North By Northwest*, Don King was about to plummet into oblivion.

King was once the most powerful promoter in boxing. And the heavyweights were his personal empire. At one point during Larry Holmes's championship reign, DK controlled eleven of the twelve top-ranked challengers in boxing's flagship division.

But that was long ago. King will be eighty-three years old on August 20, 2014. His stable of fighters has been depleted. So has his staff, as longtime lieutenants like Bobby Goodman and Alan Hopper moved on. The only fighter of note that King had left was Bermane Stiverne. And Stiverne was down on the judges' scorecards as round six of his May 10, 2014, WBC title bout against Chris Arreola began.

The fight was contested at USC's Galen Center with a meager 3,992 fans in attendance. Throughout the night, ESPN blow-by-blow announcer Joe Tessitore had spoken reverentially of the WBC belt; a trinket that writer Jimmy Tobin has labeled "the appropriately-colored slime-green alphabet strap." King had gone unmentioned during the telecast despite his on-camera presence in the second row of the technical zone.

Then, midway through round six, Stiverne landed a sweeping right hand on Arreola's temple. Chris went down, rose, was knocked down again, rose for the second time, and was helpless against the ropes when referee Jack Reiss stopped the fight.

Wladimir Klitschko (who holds the WBA, IBF, and WBO belts and is boxing's true heavyweight champion) wants to fight Stiverne to unify the belts.

Similarly, King would like Stiverne to fight Klitschko. A victory over Wladimir would give DK the heavyweight throne to bargain with.

"Don't forget," King chortled at the Stiverne-Arreola post-fight press conference. "Lamon Brewster knocked Klitschko out [in 2004, the last time that Wladimir was beaten]. That was mine, too."

But Deontay Wilder is the WBC's mandatory challenger. And Wilder is aligned with Richard Schaefer and Al Haymon. King no longer has sufficient influence to offset their power.

It would be good for boxing to have just one heavyweight champion. So whatever happens, look for it to have at least two for a while.

Meanwhile, in the ring after Stiverne-Arreola, Bermane seemed to thank everyone but Don King. That omission wouldn't have occurred during DK's glory years.

★ ★ ★

Like many boxing enthusiasts, I had hoped that newly installed WBC president Mauricio Sulaiman would build upon the accomplishments of his father but, at the same time, correct some of the abuses that have characterized the WBC for decades. That optimism was shortlived.

On June 3, 2014, I sat with Mauricio for a two-hour interview.

"The past few months have been a difficult process, very confusing," Sulaiman said at the start of our conversation. "Since my father died [on January 16, 2014], there has not been one single moment of peace for grieving and for my family. There were five thousand beautiful notes, but also immediately the calls about what do we do now. I'm very happy with the unity of the board of governors. There are many challenges because boxing today is not what it was even five years ago."

And what are those challenges?

"The WBC was formed for one main reason: to recognize who the one world champion is in every weight division," Sulaiman told me. "Everything else is second to that. That is the focus. We have to go back to basics."

So would the WBC will allow Bermane Stiverne to make the first defense of his WBC belt in a title-unification bout against Wladimir Klitschko instead of requiring him to fight Deontay Wilder?

"No," Sulaiman explained. "For the WBC to allow Klitschko to fight Stiverne for our title now would go against the IBF, which has ordered a mandatory defense for Klitschko. I cannot insult the IBF in that way."

And speaking of "one world champion in every weight division," what about all those diamond champions, silver champions, champions emeritus, etc?

"There is often a need for a championship atmosphere around a fight," Sulaiman answered.

Like father, like son.

★ ★ ★

On the night of June 14, 2014, six-time "trainer of the year" Freddie Roach was in Ruslan Provodnikov's dressing room long before the fighter arrived for his WBO 140-pound title defense against Chris Algieri.

"I'd rather be here than in the hotel," Roach said. "Hotel rooms bore me. Gyms and dressing rooms, I like."

When Roach is at home in California, he opens the Wild Card Gym in Hollywood five days a week at 7:00 am and closes it thirteen hours later. "There are times when I'm tired," he acknowledged. "But training fighters is like fighting. If you start cutting corners, it's time to quit."

The conversation turned to the relationship between trainers and fighters. "The fighter makes the trainer more than the other way around," Roach posited.

To prove his point, he cited two incidents.

"I was training in Las Vegas, getting ready to fight Tommy Cordova," Roach reminisced. "Eddie Futch was my trainer, and Ray Arcel came to visit. Eddie and Ray were friends. Eddie had told me stories about Ray for years and said that Ray was a great trainer. You had to be special for Eddie to talk about you like that."

"Ray spent a whole week in the gym with Eddie and me," Roach continued. "Then, the night of the fight [June 12, 1984], he worked my corner with Eddie. I was getting close to the end as a fighter by then. I lost a twelve-round decision. All I could say afterward was, 'I'm sorry. It was an honor to have the two of you in my corner.'"

And the other occasion?

"It was right after I quit boxing. Angelo Dundee had a fighter named Cubanito Perez, who was getting ready to fight Meldrick Taylor. Angelo was too busy to work with him. I was working as a telemarketer and was broke at the time, and Eddie suggested to Angelo that I train Perez. The fight was in Atlantic City [on July 1, 1987]. Angelo was the chief second. You had Angelo Dundee, Edde Futch, and me in the corner. And Perez lost every round."

"At the end of the day, it's about the fighter, not the trainer," Roach said. Then he added wistfully, "I'd trade all my trainer of the year awards and every dollar I've made as a trainer if I could have won a championship belt."

★ ★ ★

Floyd Mayweather showed once again in his September 13, 2014, rematch against Marcos Maidana that he's a very good fighter.

Maidana is not what Lennox Lewis used to refer to "a pugilistic specialist." He's a brawling straight-ahead fighter who, two years ago, was outboxed for ten out of ten rounds by Devon Alexander. Paulie Malignaggi once observed, "You learn in the first six months in the gym what you need to beat Maidana. After that, it's just a matter of practicing till you get it right."

In Mayweather-Maidana I, Marcos fought with passion. This time, he fought like a man who was showing up for a paycheck.

Mayweather is physically stronger than Maidana and far more skilled. On Saturday night, he kept the action in the center of the ring, controlling both distance and tempo. Also, Floyd knows how to take care of himself on the inside. He holds. He uses his forearms and elbows well. And he's a fifteen-round fighter, who tires less than his opponent as a fight goes on. Marcos seemed to tire early on Saturday night.

The only real drama came in round eight when Mayweather pushed Maidana's head down in a clinch, jammed his glove into Marcos's face, and then complained to referee Kenny Bayless that Maidana bit his glove. Two rounds later, Bayless took a point away from Marcos for using his forearm to push Floyd to the canvas in a clinch. That made the judges' final tally 116–111, 116–111, 115–112 in Floyd's favor.

In a post-fight interview, Jim Gray pressed Mayweather about fighting Manny Pacquiao in his next outing. Perhaps that reflected the unhappiness of Les Moonves (president and CEO of CBS Corporation, which owns Showtime) with another multi-million-dollar loss on a Mayweather fight.

Mayweather told Gray that he's open to the possibility. But for years, Floyd has found reasons not to fight Pacquiao.

Here, the thoughts of Sugar Ray Leonard are instructive.

"Highly anticipated fights are what made boxing what it was," Leonard said earlier this year. "When these fights don't take place, no question, it bothers me. I could not see myself not fighting Tommy Hearns. I could not see myself not fighting Roberto Duran."

Leonard, it should be noted, came out of retirement to fight Marvin Hagler.

Meanwhile, Mayweather says all the time that he's his own boss. Virtually every fighter wants to fight him because of the money involved, so Floyd can make any fight he wants happen. That's why the onus is on him if there's no Mayweather vs. Pacquiao at 147 pounds and no Mayweather vs. Gennady Golovkin at 154.

Floyd is building his legend on YouTube and Twitter. The real greats of boxing—fighters like Joe Louis, Muhammad Ali, and the two Sugar Rays (Robinson and Leonard)—fought the toughest available opposition and built their legend in the ring.

★ ★ ★

On May 4, 2013, J'Leon Love won a split-decision over Gabriel Rosado in Las Vegas to capture one of boxing's many regional belts. Then Love tested positive for hydrochlorothiazide, a banned substance that's used as a weight-loss aid and also to mask the presence of performance-enhancing drugs in a fighter's system. The result of Love-Rosado was changed to "no decision," and J'Leon was suspended for six months in addition to being fined $10,000 by the Nevada State Athletic Commission.

At his NSAC hearing, Love admitted that he'd used hydrochlorothiazide, but testified that it had been to lose weight and that he hadn't known it was illegal. He further testified that the drug had been given to him by his strength and conditioning coach, Bob Ware.

What action did the Nevada State Athletic Commission take against Ware?

Zilch. And when Floyd Mayweather fought a rematch against Marcos Maidana on September 13, one of the men in his corner (he also wrapped Floyd's hands on fight night) was Bob Ware.

★ ★ ★

There was a standing room only crowd of 9,323 at the StubHub Center in Carson, California, for the October 18, 2014, fight card featuring

Gennady Golovkin vs. Marco Antonio Rubio and Nonito Donaire vs. Nicholas Walters. Before the telecast, it was clear that Golovkin and Donaire were going in different directions. After the telecast, it was clearer.

Donaire has moved from being hailed as "the next Manny Pacquiao" and honored as the 2012 "Fighter of the Year" by the Boxing Writers Association of America to "let's reevaluate his status."

Nonito has an engaging personality. He's an exciting fighter. And he can whack. But he's technically flawed in that he (1) doesn't cut off the ring against elusive opponents as well as he should; (2) has trouble setting up his power punches unless an opponent is trading with him; and (3) often overreaches on his power shots, which leaves him vulnerable to counters.

Walters, a Jamaican knockout artist with 24 wins and 20 stoppages in 24 bouts, was expected to test Donaire. The established betting lines were close to even money on the bout.

Once the bell rang, Walters was the aggressor throughout. Donaire fought more cautiously than he usually does. When Nonito stayed on the outside, Nicholas outjabbed him. And when Donaire stopped moving to exchange, Walters outpunched him. The one bright spot for Donaire came at the end of round two. After getting hit with a low blow, Walters decided to trade low and was rocked by a hard left hook up top.

Other than that, it was all Walters. Donaire had never been knocked down before as a pro, but his glove touched the canvas for an official knockdown when he was jarred by a right uppercut at the end of round three.

Late in round six, there was a more definitive knockdown. Donaire lunged forward after overreaching on a left hook, missed, and got hit high on the back of his head behind the ear with a nasty overhand right. Nonito went down face first on the canvas and rose on unsteady legs. Referee Raul Caiz Jr appropriately stopped the fight.

"He overwhelmed me and he knocked the shit out of me," Donaire conceded afterward.

That set the stage for Golovkin-Rubio.

Golovkin is the World Boxing Association "super" middleweight champion. Danny Jacobs holds a bogus WBA "world middleweight championship" belt.

Rubio had won the vacant World Boxing Council "interim world middleweight championship" in April of this year by beating Domenico Spada of Italy. Spada qualified for that "championship" bout by beating Sandor Ramocsa (12 wins in 33 fights), Norbert Szekeres (13 wins in 40 fights), and Marijan Markovic (4 wins in 25 fights) during the preceding twenty-one months.

Prior to Golovkin-Rubio, the WBC announced that it was sanctioning the bout for its "interim world middleweight championship." That sanction meant the WBC could enrich its coffers by collecting another sanctioning fee. Rubio then showed his respect for the belt by weighing in 1.8 pounds over the 160-pound limit.

Going into the fight, Golovkin's record stood at 30 and 0 with 27 knockouts. Rubio's ring ledger showed 59 wins, 6 losses, and 3 draws. Marco Antonio had won a couple of rounds in going the distance in a losing effort against Julio Cesar Chavez Jr in 2012. Three years before that, in his only other world championship bid, he was knocked out in nine rounds by Kelly Pavlik. The odds favoring Golovkin over Rubio were in the range of 50 to 1.

In the ring, Gennady always seems to be in control. This time was no different. Prior to the bout, Jimmy Tobin labeled the match-up a "sanctioned slaughter" and noted, "You can hit Golovkin. That much has been established. Taking what he offers in return thus far has proven too much to ask."

That was certainly true of Golovkin-Rubio. Midway through round one, Rubio had tasted enough of Golovkin's power that he was noticeably less aggressive than he'd been in the opening minute of the bout. By the midway mark of round two, it was over, courtesy of a left hook that landed high on Marco Antonio's temple and deposited him on the canvas for a ten count.

Miguel Cotto is currently the WBC "world middleweight champion." In theory, Golovkin is now the mandatory challenger for Cotto's belt.

The chances that Cotto will fight Golovkin are about as good as the chances that New Jersey governor Chris Christie will run a sub-four-minute mile. Cotto will avoid Golovkin. And the WBC will sanction Cotto's next bout (which will be against someone else for some form of WBC championship). The WBC will say that this is for "the good of boxing." Of course, a substantial sanctioning fee will be involved.

So let's simply say that, right now, Gennady Golovkin is the best middleweight in the world. Anyone else who claims to be a "world champion" at 160 pounds is a pretender.

★ ★ ★

Floyd Mayweather prides himself on his defense. But as of late, "Money" has taken some hits outside the ring.

During a "satellite tour" two days before Mayweather-Maidana II, Floyd was interviewed by Rachel Nichols on CNN. Nichols ground him to pieces over the issue of domestic violence and Mayweather's multiple convictions for what she called his "brutal history" of physically abusing women.

Floyd tried to deflect the issue, saying, "Everything has been allegations. Nothing has been proven."

But unlike the enablers who have approved, sanctioned, and televised Mayweather's fights in recent years, Nichols engaged, noting, "In the incident you went to jail for, the mother of your three children did show some bruising [and] a concussion when she went to the hospital. It was your own kids who called the police, gave them a detailed description of the abuse. There has been documentation."

"Umm," Floyd responded. "Once again . . . Ahh . . . No pictures; just hearsay and allegations, and I signed a plea bargain. So once again, not true."

Then Nichols landed another power punch.

"But the website *Deadspin* recently detailed seven separate physical assaults on five different women that resulted in arrest or citation. Are we really supposed to believe all these women are lying, including the incidents when there were witnesses like your own kids?"

"Everybody actually . . . Ummm . . . Everybody is entitled to their own opinion. You know, when it's all said and done, only God can judge me."

Mayweather's fumbling of the ball again on the issue of domestic violence followed another embarrassment—a series of exchanges with Curtis Jackson aka 50 Cent.

Last month, the rapper offered to donate $750,000 to a charity of Mayweather's choosing if Floyd could read a full page from a Harry Potter book without a flub. Later, 50 Cent amended the offer to Mayweather, saying, "I got a phone call from my man, Jimmy Kimmel. Jimmy said he'll put it on the actual show. We don't want to put pressure on you. We know you can't pronounce those words in the Harry Potter book, so we're going to let you read *Cat in the Hat*."

Soon after, a tape of Floyd reading a promo for *The Breakfast Club* off a teleprompter surfaced. He did not do well.

That leads to the question of whether or not Mayweather's archrival, Manny Pacquiao, can read *Harry Potter*. After all, Pacquiao grew up in abject poverty, living at times on the streets in the Philippines.

A telephone call to publicist Fred Sternburg (who has spent years with Pacquiao) seemed in order.

"Not only can Manny read Harry Potter," Sternburg informed this writer. "He can read Harry Potter in English and Tagalog."

★ ★ ★

I've always liked Shannon Briggs. He was a solid fighter in his day and acquitted himself well in some significant fights.

There are far too many "champions" in boxing and have been for some time. That said; I understood where Briggs was coming from when he proclaimed, "I feel like I've been successful in boxing. I didn't achieve the status of a Mike Tyson or a Lennox Lewis, but I'm happy with what I achieved. Coming from where I came from, homeless in Brooklyn, sleeping in shelters, everything I did was an accomplishment. I don't care what anyone else says. I made good; I'm proud of what I've accomplished. And I was the lineal heavyweight champion of the world whether people like it or not."

Briggs's last hurrah was a brutal twelve-round beating that he absorbed at the hands of Vitali Klitschko in 2010. He showed incredible courage and fortitude in going the distance that night. Nothing good has happened to him in boxing since then.

After four years away from the ring, Briggs returned in 2014 and had four wins against opponents who weren't even good club fighters. Now, at age forty-three, he's pursuing a fight against Wladimir Klitschko.

In an effort to land the Klitschko fight, Shannon has incessantly stalked the champion. He invaded Klitschko's training camp, aggressively interrupted Wladimir when the latter was eating lunch in a restaurant, and, more recently, rented a speedboat in order to knock Klitschko off a surfboard when Wladimir was paddling off the coast of Hollywood, Florida.

This is how tragedies happen. Tempers rise. Things can get out of hand.

It's uncertain what will happen next. Briggs seems inclined to engage in more antics. Klitschko may well be forced to go to court and ask for a protective order to safeguard himself and those around him.

What's particularly sad is that Shannon once had a grace and dignity about him. Those qualities appear to be gone now.

★ ★ ★

Lloyd Price was at the Belvedere Hotel in Manhattan this past Monday [September 15, 2014] to tape an interview for a PBS documentary about Muhammad Ali that will air in 2015.

Price, who was inducted into the Rock and Roll Hall of Fame in 1998, met Cassius Clay in Louisville in 1958. "Stagger Lee" (which Price recorded) had just become the first rock-and-roll song sung by a black recording artist to reach #1 on the *Billboard* charts.

"I was on tour," Price told me years ago when I was researching *Muhammad Ali: His Life and Times*. "Ali was sixteen years old, sitting outside the Top Hat Lounge because he was underage and they wouldn't let him in. When I got to the lounge, this crazy kid rushed over, saying, 'Mr. Price, I'm Cassius Marcellus Clay; I'm the Golden Gloves Champion of Louisville, Kentucky; someday I'm gonna be heavyweight champion of the world; I love your music; and I'm gonna be famous like you.' I just looked at him, and said, 'Kid, you're dreaming.' But we got along. You couldn't help but like him. The Top Hat Lounge was a popular place, and each time I played there, I saw him. After a while, I started looking for him and bringing him in with me. He had all sorts of questions—about music and traveling, but mostly he wanted to know about girls. There were a lot of things he didn't know, and he asked me how to make out with girls. He was very sincere about it. I told him, 'Just be yourself, and the girls will like you.' Although as part of the lesson, I gave him a couple of dollars and said, 'Always have some money. That's the beginning of hanging out with the foxes.'"

Price is eighty-one years old now and thinner than the last time I saw him. At the Belvedere Hotel, he was walking with a cane. But his voice was clear; there was a gleam in his eye; and his contagious laugh filled the room. The taping lasted just under an hour, and the memories flowed.

"I took a real liking to Cassius. I was number one then, and he'd ask me, 'What does it feel like to be a big star'... You have to remember what America was like at that time. In parts of the country, I'm being booked into white clubs. I'm being booked to do white dances. But I can't stay at the white hotel, and I have to go around to the back door if I want a sandwich . . . I went to some [Nation of Islam] meetings with Ali. For the first time in my life—as a grown man who was a star who had sold millions of records—I heard somebody saying, 'You are somebody.' The language gave you such a lift. You left feeling good about yourself. In the end, it wasn't my thing. But I can understand how Ali got hooked . . . Ali's heart is pure. He was always true to himself . . . Ali had no problem with being a black man."

★ ★ ★

Boxing puts its best foot forward with good fights inside the ring. Every so often, something outside the ring also gives its partisans reason to be proud.

On August 10, 2014, Frank Maloney (who was once among the ranks of England's leading managers and promoters) announced that he had been living as a woman for the past year and was undergoing gender reassignment.

"I was born in the wrong body and I have always known I was a woman," Maloney told *The Mirror.* "I can't keep living in the shadows. That is why I am doing what I am today. Living with the burden any longer would have killed me. What was wrong at birth is now being medically corrected. I have a female brain. I knew I was different from the minute I could compare myself to other children. I wasn't in the right body."

Maloney's revelation was greeted with demeaning comments in some circles. But overall, the boxing community has responded with tolerance and compassion. Lennox Lewis, who became heavyweight champion of the world under Maloney's guidance, spoke for his brethren when he posted the following statement on his Facebook page:

"I was just as shocked as anyone at the news about my former promoter. My initial thought was that it was a wind up. The great thing about life, and boxing, is that, day to day, you never know what to expect. This world we live in isn't always cut and dried or black and white. Coming from the boxing fraternity, I can only imagine what a difficult decision this must be for Kellie [Maloney's new name]. However, having taken some time to read Kellie's statements, I understand better what she and others in similar situations are going through. I think that ALL people should be allowed to live their lives in a way that brings them harmony and inner peace."

★ ★ ★

Words of Wisdom from Great Fighters

Jack Johnson: When you look into a man's eyes, you can almost always tell when he's going to attack or is getting ready to throw a punch. Through much experience, I can even guess what type of punch and defend myself accordingly. I don't understand how this sort of mental transmission takes place. I use the advantage it gives me and leave the task of explaining it to people smarter than I.

Max Baer: I figure the fight game like this. I'm a puncher. I can knock them over with either hand. I figure the smartest of them will get careless once in ten rounds. That's all I ask. Let him slip up once and I've got him.

Jimmy McLarnin: If you think I was great, you should have seen Harry Greb.

★ ★ ★

On April 17, 1860, in Farnsborough County west of London, England's Tom Sayers and John Heenan of San Francisco fought to a bloody forty-two-round draw in what was then called "The Fight of the Century." Late in the contest, Sayers was barely able to defend himself, while Heenan was blind in one eye and his other eye was rapidly closing.

Commenting on the scene, New York tavern owner and boxing entrepreneur Harry Hill observed, "Heenan tried to laugh two or three times after Sayers had cut him bad. But upon my soul, his face was so out of shape, you couldn't tell whether he was laughing or crying."

Fighters absorb punishment in the ring. That's the reality of boxing. After Sam Langford was knocked out by Harry Wills, the beaten fighter explained, "You know, iron breaks now and then. And my jaw ain't iron."

Sonny Liston said of his profession, "Fighting ain't fun. It's like war. If I could do something else, I would. I don't like earning my living getting hurt."

Lennox Lewis put matters in perspective when asked recently if he misses being an active fighter.

"That's like asking a guy if he misses getting punched in his face," Lennox answered.

★ ★ ★

And a bit more on the Brits—

If British boxing writing in the nineteenth century belonged to Pierce Egan, then the twentieth century was the domain of Hugh McIlvanney. Herewith, a few quotes from each man.

★ Pierce Egan: "No men are more subject to the caprice or changes of fortune than pugilists. Victory brings them fame, riches, and patrons. Their bruises are not heeded in the smiles of success. Basking in the sunshine of prosperity, their lives pass on pleasantly until defeat comes and reverses the scene. Then, covered with aches and pains, distressed in mind and body, assailed by poverty, wretchedness, and misery; their friends forsake them. Their towering fame expired and no longer the plaything of fashion, they fly to inebriation for relief and a premature end puts a period to their misfortunes."

* Hugh McIlvanney [on the possible use of headgear and other protective measures in professional boxing]: "If the game loses its rawness, it is nothing. If it ever became a kind of fencing with fists, a mere trial of skills, reflexes, and agility, and not the test of courage, will, and resilience that it is now, it would lose its appeal."

* Pierce Egan: "It seems scarcely possible that any man can die in possession of the championship unless he dies young."

* Hugh McIlvanney: "Professional boxing is the most truly egalitarian of sports; a world in which great champions and obscure journeymen are equally exposed to barefaced robbery."

★ ★ ★

I go to Las Vegas once or twice a year for fights. When I was young, a "good night" in Las Vegas was hanging out with a hot woman. Now it's getting eight hours sleep.

I was in the media center at the MGM Grand, talking with Floyd Mayweather Sr the day before his son's September 14, 2013, fight against Canelo Alvarez.

I think that Floyd Jr is a superb boxer. I don't think that he merits inclusion on the short list of all-time greats because he has consistently ducked the toughest available opposition and therefore failed to prove himself against the best competition that boxing has to offer.

I asked Floyd Sr, "Who ranks as the greater fighter? Your son or Muhammad Ali?"

"Ali," Mayweather said without hesitation. "I loved to watch Ali fight. I didn't like the Muslim part and the hate that came with it. But the way Ali fought, that was beautiful. And he stood up for his people. I would have done it a little different. But he did it, and I didn't. What he did will never happen again in the ring. Not outside the ring either."

The sports memorabilia industry has far too many questionable practices. This article highlighted one of them.

The SCP Summer Premier Auction

August 23, 2014, was the final day of bidding for SCP's "Summer Premier Auction."

SCP Auctions was founded in 1979 and is one of the largest auctioneers and private sellers of sports memorabilia in the United States. Its past sales have included:

★ A T206 Honus Wagner tobacco card graded PSA NM-MT 8—$2,800,000

★ A Babe Ruth game-worn (circa 1920) road jersey—$4,415,000

★ The bat (later signed by Ruth) that Babe Ruth used on April 18, 1923, to hit the first home run in Yankee Stadium—$1,265,000

★ The contract for the sale of Babe Ruth from the Boston Red Sox to the New York Yankees—$996,000

★ The ball hit by Barry Bonds for career home run #756, breaking Hank Aaron's all-time home run record—$752,467

Where the sweet science is concerned, SCP auctioned off "The Angelo Dundee Collection" of boxing memorabilia in November 2012 for more than $1,300,000. Two pairs of gloves worn by Cassius Clay, later known as Muhammad Ali, in his first fight against Sonny Liston and his first fight against Joe Frazier sold for $385,848 each.

That brings us to SCP's 2014 Summer Premier Auction. Fifty-nine boxing-related items were on the block. Some of them are cause for concern.

Let's start with the following as described by SCP in its auction catalog:

★ Lot #114: "Willie Pep's 1940's training worn gloves and Everlast head gear"

★ Lot #112: "c.1942 Willie Pep fight worn Everlast boxing gloves"

★ Lot #115: "November 6, 1957, Alphonse Halimi fight worn Ben Lee boxing gloves—15 round decision vs. Raton Macias"

★ Lot #95: "c.1910 Jim Jeffries fight worn Everlast boxing shoes"

Craig Hamilton is the foremost boxing memorabilia dealer in the United States. Over the years, he has been retained by Sotheby's, Christie's, Heritage, and numerous other auction houses to document and authenticate memorabilia prior to auction.

This writer reached out to Hamilton, who had this to say about the items listed above:

★ [Lot #114, which sold for $720] "The Everlast label on the head gear has an 'R' with a circle around it to protect the Everlast trademark. Everlast didn't add that 'R' to its headgear until 1966. That means the headgear couldn't possibly have been worn by Pep in the 1940s."

★ [Lot #112, which sold for $1,320] "These gloves were made by Everlast and stamped '24 14,' which indicates that they're 14-ounce gloves. Pep wore 6-ounce gloves in fights."

★ [Lot #115, which sold for $1,253] "This was a tough fifteen-round fight. The gloves Halimi wore were heavily taped above the label, which is shown in the pictures that SCP has on its website. Anybody who knows anything about boxing memorabilia and stopped to think about it would know that these aren't the gloves Halimi wore in that fight. The real gloves would show some tape residue or leather-surface removal after fifteen rounds of sweat and the like."

★ [Lot #95, which sold for $1,200]: "These are supposed to be fight-worn Jim Jeffries boxing shoes that have an Everlast label inside them. Initially, SCP described them as being 'circa 1900.' Then it learned that Everlast didn't come into existence until 1910, so it added an addendum to the catalog saying that the shoes were 'circa 1910.' The problem with that is, Everlast didn't make boxing equipment in 1910. They started making it in 1917, long after Jeffries's career was over."

There's more.

Lot #102 purports to be a "c.1926 Gene Tunney 'The Fighting Marine' fight worn boxing robe." It sold for $15,052.

"How do they know that Tunney wore this robe in a fight?" Hamilton asks. "Over the years, I've looked at every film of Gene Tunney in the ring that I could find. I have 200-to-300 photos of Tunney in the ring before and after fights. And I've I never seen him standing in the ring wearing a robe. Every image I've seen shows him wearing a towel over his shoulders, not a robe."

"And I have problems with some of the other items," Hamilton continues. "Lots 100 and 101 purport to be the gloves that Jack Dempsey wore in his 1918 fight against Fred Fulton and his 1927 fight against Jack Sharkey. They're autographed by Dempsey. The first pair sold for $18,840; the second pair for $22,796. I don't question that the handwriting is Dempsey's. But Dempsey was a prolific giver-away of boxing memorabilia that wasn't what he said it was. He'd give something to someone and tell them it was something that it wasn't to make them feel good."

Each of the auction items referenced above came with a Letter of Provenance stating that it had been in the "Helms Athletic Foundation/ LA84 Collection." The Helms Athletic Foundation was created in 1936 and went through several incarnations before being dissolved and its holdings absorbed into the Amateur Athletic Foundation (renamed the LA84 Foundation in 2007).

"Just because these pieces were in something called the Helms Athletic Foundation collection doesn't mean that they're real," Hamilton says. "There's no indication that experts were used to authenticate any of the boxing items in the collection with the exception of PSA/DNA for autographs. Did these guys look at old fight films? Did they look at old photos? Did they weigh the gloves or contact Everlast? Essentially, they're saying that, because these items came from the Helms Athletic Foundation, that authenticates them. This is an old auction practice, but it doesn't cut it today. There are several items in the auction that can't possibly be what SCP says they are. So what does that say about the other items in the auction? I'm sure that most of them are authentic, but I would speculate that some aren't."

SCP vice president Dan Imler acknowledged to this writer that SCP didn't hire an outside expert to authenticate the boxing memorabilia in its 2014 Summer Premier Auction.

"That's something we do on a case by case basis," Imler said. "Here, we didn't think it was necessary because we relied on the Helms archives and its records for authentication. We take authentication very seriously, but we're not perfect. If there are problems, we'll notify the purchasers and make whatever corrections need to be made."

Meanwhile, Hamilton has no plans to pursue the matter. "I'm not the auction police," he says. "But I hate it when stuff like this happens."

One might add that SCP isn't some hustler selling phony memorabilia on eBay, where the prevailing ethos is "buyer beware." To quote the SCP website, "SCP Auctions, one of the nation's largest auctioneers and private sellers of important sports memorabilia and cards, is a leader in the industry."

Floyd Mayweather's partisans maintain that he's the greatest fighter of all time. The experts disagree.

Mayweather and Pacquiao vs. the Modern 135-Pound Greats

Last year, I coordinated a poll in which industry experts predicted the outcome of a fantasy round-robin tournament at 147 pounds. Floyd Mayweather and Manny Pacquiao were among the participants. The runaway winner was Sugar Ray Robinson. Ray Leonard finished in second place.

Since then, numerous readers have asked how the experts think Mayweather and Pacquiao would have fared against the lightweight greats.

The answer follows.

The eight fighters chosen for the 135-pound fantasy round-robin tournament in alphabetical order are: Julio Cesar Chavez, Roberto Duran, Juan Manuel Marquez, Floyd Mayweather, Shane Mosley, Carlos Ortiz, Manny Pacquiao, and Pernell Whitaker.

Legendary greats Joe Gans, Benny Leonard, Tony Canzoneri, and Henry Armstrong weren't included because there's not enough available film footage to properly evaluate them. Ike Williams was also a bit before the cutoff date.

Issues such as same-day weigh-ins versus day-before weigh-ins might be considered by purists. And there's a difference between going twelve rounds as opposed to fifteen. But at the end of the day, either a fighter is very good, great, or the greatest.

All of the fighters chosen for the tournament also fought at one time or another at weights other than 135 pounds. The electors were asked to assume for purposes of their predictions that each fighter was duplicating his best 135-pound performance.

Twenty-six experts participated in the rankings process. Listed alphabetically, the panelists were:

Trainers: Teddy Atlas, Pat Burns, Naazim Richardson, and Don Turner

Media: Al Bernstein, Steve Farhood, Harold Lederman, Paulie Malignaggi, Dan Rafael, and Michael Rosenthal

Matchmakers: Eric Bottjer, Don Elbaum, Bobby Goodman, Brad Goodman, Ron Katz, Mike Marchionte, Chris Middendorf, Russell Peltz, and Bruce Trampler.

Historians: Craig Hamilton, Don McRae, Bob Mee, Clay Moyle, Adam Pollack, Randy Roberts, and Mike Tyson

That's right! Mike Tyson. Mike is a serious historian when it comes to boxing. His input was very much valued.

If each of the eight fighters listed above had fought the other seven, there would have been twenty-eight fights. And there were twenty-six panelists. Thus, 728 fights were entered in the data base.

Fighters were awarded one point for each predicted win and a half-point for each predicted draw (too close to call).

A perfect score (each voter predicting that the same fighter would win every one of his fights) would have been 182 points.

"Styles make fights," one elector cautioned. "But it's more than that. You don't know for sure how these guys would have fought each other and what adjustments they would have made during the course of each fight."

That said; the results have been tabulated. The rankings are:

Roberto Duran	164.5 points
Pernell Whitaker	133.5
Floyd Mayweather	122.0
Julio Cesar Chavez	102.5
Shane Mosley	71.0
Carlos Ortiz	53.5
Manny Pacquiao	48.5
Juan Manuel Marquez	32.5

Fifteen of the twenty-six electors ranked Duran #1. Four electors ranked Mayweather #1. Three electors ranked Whitaker #1. One elector (a matchmaker) ranked Ortiz #1. In addition, two electors had Duran and Whitaker tied for first place. One elector had Duran, Whitaker, and Mayweather in a three-way tie.

Fourteen electors gave Duran a perfect score (that is, winning all seven of his fights). Whitaker and Mayweather received three perfect scores and Ortiz one.

Chart #1 and Chart #2 contain underlying statistical data from the tournament.

Name Total Points	Overall Rank	Matchmaker Rank	Trainer Rank	Media Rank	Historian Rank
Duran 164.5	1	1	1	1	1
Whitaker 133.5	2	2	2	2	3
Mayweather 122.0	3	3	3	3	2
Chavez 102.5	4	4	4	4	4
Mosley 71.0	5	5	5	5	6
Ortiz 53.5	6	6	6	6	8
Pacquiao 48.5	7	8	7	7	5
Marquez 32.5	8	7	8	8	7

Chart #1 shows that, by and large, the matchmakers, trainers, media representatives, and historians saw things similarly. Duran was ranked #1 within each group of electors. The trainer and media rankings were identical to the final consensus. Mayweather and Pacquiao fared slightly better among historians than among other groups.

	Duran	Whitaker	Mayweather	Chavez	Mosley	Ortiz	Pacquiao	Marquez
Duran 160-13-9	—	18.5	20.5	24.5	24.5	25	26	25.5
Whitaker 127-42-13	7.5	—	15.5	21.5	19.5	22	23	24.5
Mayweather 117-55-10	5.5	10.5	—	15	21.5	21.5	24	24
Chavez 96-73-13	1.5	4.5	11	—	17	20.5	24	24
Mosley 68-108-6	1.5	6.5	4.5	9	—	16	13	20.5
Ortiz 52-127-3	1	4	4.5	5.5	10	—	12	16.5
Pacquiao 45-130-7	0	3	2	2	13	14	—	14.5
Marquez 28-145-9	.5	1.5	2	2	5.5	9.5	11.5	—

Chart #2 shows the composite won-lost record for each fighter and how the panelists thought each fighter would fare against the other seven.

Roberto Duran was regarded as the cream of the crop.

"People have forgotten how good Duran was at 135-pounds," one elector noted. "He was an excellent defensive fighter with a savage attack and he could punch."

Pernell Whitaker was the consensus choice for #2. "He was a defensive wizard," another elector said. "He punched harder than people gave him credit for. And the fact that he was a southpaw made it even harder to figure him out."

Floyd Mayweather ranked third.

"I don't question Floyd's skills," an elector who thought Mayweather would win only three of seven fights in the tournament observed. "But all the other guys on this list relished the challenge of going in tough. Floyd might not have had the heart to win the fights in this tournament.

We don't know how he would have handled the pressure against fighters of this caliber."

Some of the fights in the 135-pound fantasy tournament happened in real life. Mayweather and Pacquiao fought Mosley and Marquez. Whitaker and Chavez did battle. But none of these fights were contested at 135 pounds and, in most instances, one of the combatants was past his prime.

That answers the question of how four electors could pick Mosley over Mayweather at 135 pounds with one more calling the fight too close to call. "They fought at 147 pounds," an elector explains. "And Shane was an old man (38 years old) by then. Shane was much better at 135 pounds than he was at the higher weights. And Floyd wasn't as good at 135 as he is at 147."

Meanwhile, it's important to remember that each of the fighters in this tournament merits recognition as a terrific fighter. On a given night, any one of them might have beaten the others.

The New York Times *is a great newspaper. But it's falling short of its mission insofar as its coverage of boxing is concerned.*

100 Days: The *New York Times* and Boxing

Five years ago, I wrote an article entitled "The New York Times and Boxing." I catalogued every article that appeared in the paper's sports section over a one-hundred-day period and concluded, "The *New York Times* no longer covers boxing as an ongoing sport. If a fighter of importance dies, it's noted. On rare occasions, bouts are referenced. But the paper's motto—'All the News That's Fit to Print'—which is prominently displayed in the upper-lefthand corner of page one each day, doesn't extend to boxing."

The response to the article was gratifying. Tom Jolly (then the *Times* sports editor) invited Larry Merchant and myself to breakfast to discuss ways that the *Times* might improve its boxing coverage. In due course, Greg Bishop became the paper's go-to boxing guy. Coverage of the sweet science wasn't extensive, but at least the *Times* recognized boxing.

Now the pendulum has swung again. In 2011, Jolly was promoted to associate managing editor. He was succeeded as sports editor by Joe Sexton, who gave way in January 2013 to Jason Stallman. Earlier this year, Greg Bishop left the paper to take a job with *Sports Illustrated*. Since Bishop's departure, boxing has all but disappeared from the *Times*.

In May of this year (2014), I decided to repeat my exercise of five years ago. From May 19 through August 26, I tracked every article that appeared in the print edition of the *Times* that's distributed in New York.

The conclusion: The *New York Times* no longer covers boxing as an ongoing sport. If a fighter of importance dies, it's noted. On rare occasions, bouts are referenced. But the paper's motto—"All the News That's Fit to Print"—which is prominently displayed in the upper-lefthand corner of page one each day, doesn't extend to boxing.

Only things are worse now than they were five years ago. During the one-hundred-day period surveyed in 2009, there were seven full articles about boxing and nineteen short news "briefings." During the one-hundred-day period surveyed this year, there was only one full article about boxing in the *Times* sports section and four "briefings."

Let's look at the statistical data.

Certain events demanded significant coverage during the hundred days in question. These included the ongoing Major League Baseball Season, the National Basketball Association and National Hockey League playoffs, the World Cup, three major golf tournaments (the US Open, British Open, and PGA), three major tennis tournaments (the French Open, Wimbledon, and the start of the US Open), the National Football League pre-season, the Belmont Stakes, and LeBron James signing with the Cleveland Cavaliers.

The statistical summary is as follows:

	Full Story	Short Item
Major League Baseball	326	883
Soccer	242	105
NBA Basketball	148	38
Tennis	120	39
Golf	99	61
NFL Football	67	188
Hockey	66	31
Horse Racing	50	14
Cycling	29	5
Miscellaneous Business	26	5
Auto Racing	13	30
College Football	12	26
Track and Field	10	22
Swimming	16	9
Little League Baseball	16	2
WNBA Basketball	3	26
Olympics	4	7
College Basketball	4	10
College Baseball	3	11
Rugby	2	2

Lacrosse	2	2
Skateboarding	2	—
Hunting and Fishing	2	—
Triathlon	2	—
BOXING	**1**	**4**
Gymnastics	1	2
Surfing	1	1
Rock Climbing	1	—
Field Hockey	1	—
Cricket	1	—
Muoy Boran	1	—
Sumo Wrestling	1	—
Bocce	1	—
Squash	1	—
Diving for Abalone	1	—
Sailing	—	4
Figure Skating	—	2
Mixed Martial Arts	—	2

This statistical summary doesn't include the *Times'* daily recital of Major League Baseball standings, box scores of every Major League Baseball game, Major League Baseball league leaders in individual categories, Major League Soccer standings, WNBA standings, round-by-round leader boards for golf tournaments, round-by-round match results from tennis tournaments played all over the world, and statistical summaries for every NBA and NHL playoff game.

The summary shows that Major League Baseball received the most extensive coverage in the *Times*, followed by soccer, NBA basketball, tennis, and golf.

There were ten fight cards of note televised by HBO and Showtime during the survey period. The dates and featured fight on each card were:

May 24	Adonis Stevenson vs. Andrzej Fonfara
May 31	Carl Froch vs. George Groves
June 7	Miguel Cotto vs. Sergio Martinez
June 14	Ruslan Provodnikov vs. Chris Algieri
June 21	Vasyl Lomachenko vs. Gary Russell Jr

June 28   Terence Crawford vs. Yuriorkis Gamboa
July 12   Canelo Alvarez vs. Erislandy Lara
July 26   Gennady Golovkin vs. Daniel Geale
August 9   Danny Garcia vs. Rod Salka
August 16   Shawn Porter vs. Kell Brook

Four of these cards took place in New York (two at Madison Square Garden and two at Barclays Center).

The *Times* ignored all but one of the above fight cards. The only coverage of boxing in the sports section during the entire hundred-day period was:

★ June 1, 2014: One column-inch on Nonito Donaire's technical-decision victory over Simpiwe Vetyeka in Macau.

★ June 9: Three column-inches on Oscar De La Hoya, Felix Trinidad, and Joe Calzaghe being inducted into the International Boxing Hall of Fame in Canastota.

★ June 13: An article about Chris Algieri.

★ June 16: One column-inch on Algieri's victory over Ruslan Provodnikov.

★ July 18: A one column-inch item reporting that Cashmere Jackson (a twenty-six-year-old former women's light-welterweight amateur boxing champion) died in Cleveland after jumping onto the roof of a car that an assailant drove toward her after an altercation.

The Cashmere Jackson report epitomized the *Times*'s attitude toward boxing. It appeared during the same week that Floyd Mayweather and Marcos Maidana were engaged in a national tour to promote their September 13, 2014, rematch. The *Times* had no coverage of the tour. Instead, it chose to single out an ugly incident involving a fringe participant in boxing.

In addition to the above pieces, the *Times* also ran an obituary on Matthew Saad Muhammad in the obituary section on May 28. An article about Gennady Golovkin making a walk-on appearance in the Broadway musical version of *Rocky* appeared in the news section (not sports) on July 23.

Most egregiously, the *Times* didn't devote one word of coverage to the June 7 middleweight championship fight between Miguel Cotto and Sergio Martinez at Madison Square Garden. However, one day before the fight, it saw fit to tell its readers that the Edmonton Eskimos of the Canadian Football League had released Joe Adams. And on the day of the fight, it printed the second-round results from the Manulife Financial Classic woman's golf tournament in Waterloo, Ontario. For those who are interested, Shanhan Feng and Hee Young Park were tied for the lead in Ontario at 11 under par.

What else did the *Times* cover?

On June 28, Terence Crawford had a thrilling breakout performance against Yuriorkis Gamboa. The *Times* never mentioned the fight. Perhaps it was too late for the Sunday edition. But it wasn't mentioned on Monday either, when the *Times* devoted 204 column inches to sumo wrestling.

On July 26, Gennady Golovkin made an emphatic statement at Madison Square Garden with a third-round knockout of Daniel Geale. The *Times* sports section didn't mention the fight the following day. But it did feature 340 column inches on diving for abalone off the coast of California.

The *Times* also devoted more space in single articles to the World Muay Boran Federation martial arts championships in Ayutthaya, Thailand (120 column inches on May 19), bocce (120 column inches on May 26), the University of Tokyo baseball team (100 column inches on June 15), bluefish fishing near Sheepshead Bay (120 column inches on July 17), rock climbing (148 column inches on August 19), cricket (72 column inches on August 21), and rugby (136 column inches on August 25) than it did to boxing during the entire one-hundred-day survey period.

Here's a sampling of what the *Times* (which didn't consider Cotto-Martinez worthy of mention) did consider newsworthy: Round-by-round results of matches from various men's tennis tournaments, including the Topshelf Open in Den Bosch, the Bet-At-Home Open in Hamburg, the Claro Open in Bogota, and the Croatia Open in Umag. Also, round-by-round results of matches from various women's tennis tournaments, including the Aegon Classic at the Edgbaston Priory Club in Birmingham, England; the Gastien Open in Bad Gastein, Austria; the Bucharest Open in Bucharest, Romania; and the Baku Cup in Baku, Azerbaijan. It also listed the top three finishers in track and field events at the Golden Spike Meet in Ostrava in the Czech Republic.

There was no report on the outcome of Carl Froch vs. George Groves.
But at various times during the survey period, the *Times* informed its
readers that the New Jersey Institute of Technology would not renew
the contract of men's volleyball coach Ryan McNeil or strength and
conditioning coach Dan Hill; Blake Metcalf was the new video coordinator at Albany College; Amy Simon had been named women's lacrosse
coach at Fredonia College; Brett Harker was the new pitching coach
at Furman; Ray Cameron had resigned as women's lacrosse coach at
Lees-McRae College; Sean Raffile was the new swimming coach at
Bridgeport College; Brendan Armstrong had been promoted from coordinator of athletic services to director of campus recreation at Lasalle;
Brian McCullough was the new pitching coach and recruiting coordinator at Sienna College; Rachel Carey was the new assistant volleyball
coach at Baruch College; Michael Graves was the new assistant soft-
ball coach at Carson-Newman College; Tanya Kotowicz was the new
women's lacrosse coach at Central Connecticut State; Karl DeHof had
been named coordinator of compliance at Limestone College; Darryce
Moore was the new assistant women's basketball coach at Martin
Methodist College; and Lucas Monroe was the new assistant strength
and conditioning coach at Texas-Pan American College.

There's more.

The *Times* also noted that Caroline King and Samantha Sarff had
been named assistant women's rowing coaches at Clemson; Megan
Corrigan was the new assistant women's lacrosse coach at Susquehanna
College; Joe Schoen and Brandon Misiaszek had been named assistant
men's lacrosse coaches at Utica College; Jordan Smith was the new assistant men's tennis coach at Middle Tennessee College; Allen Corbin had
resigned as assistant men's basketball coach at Shenandoah College; John
Maine had been named volunteer assistant basketball coach at Charlotte
College; Justin Barker was the new assistant women's volleyball coach at
Loyola of New Orleans; and Jason Cichowicz was the new assistant athletic director for ticketing operations at Delaware College.

Jason Stallman, as earlier noted, is the *New York Times sports* editor.
He's a respected journalist, who began working for the paper in 2003,
became deputy sports editor in 2010, and assumed his present position
in January 2013.

Speaking with the *Columbia Journalism Review*, Stallman declared, "We want to give our readers something noticeably different. We try to be imaginative and experimental. That could be in the form of story topic, design, photography, graphics, whatever. Just something that doesn't feel like everything else out there."

When asked by this writer to outline the philosophy that drives the sports department, Stallman responded, "We just try to cover the world of sports in an aggressive and imaginative way. We try to tell different stories in different ways. We try to cover the events that our readers are most interested in. It's an incredibly inexact science."

Stallman also acknowledged placing greater emphasis on traditionally European sports like soccer and cycling than his predecessors did.

"Our audience is more and more global," he explained. "We have readers all over the world—a lot of them—so we've expanded our reporting in that direction."

Of course, one might note that boxing is a global sport. And the *Times* didn't have one word of coverage on Carl Froch vs. George Groves, which attracted 80,000 fans to Wembley Stadium.

Stallman has never been to a professional fight. Asked how often he watches boxing on television, he answered, "When I was a kid, I was enchanted by Hagler, Leonard, Duran, Barkley, Mugabi, Spinks, Hearns. But I have a hard time watching it, considering everything we've learned in recent years about the long-term effects of repeated brain trauma. It's just a little too jarring for me."

Football is jarring too. But the *Times* offers saturation coverage of the National Football League and college football for five months each year.

The lack of boxing coverage in the *Times* is frustrating for fans and also for people who make their living in the sweet science. Some of the best-established sports brands in New York—Madison Square Garden, HBO, Barclays Center, Showtime—are associated with boxing. Miguel Cotto vs. Sergio Martinez set a record for the largest live attendance for a boxing match in the history of Madison Square Garden. One million viewers watched Gennady Golovkin vs. Daniel Geale live on HBO. The *Times* covers events that don't come close to matching those numbers. By way of example; the average television audience for a New Jersey Devils hockey game is fifteen thousand households. A Major League

Soccer game doesn't generate anything near the on-site attendance or live television audience that a big fight does. But these games are covered regularly by the *Times*.

It's also troubling that, at present, the *Times* couldn't cover complex boxing issues on short notice if it wanted to. The biggest stories in the sport often occur behind the scenes. And no one now at the *Times* knows what's going on behind the scenes in boxing. The paper simply doesn't have a "go to" person on staff who's grounded in the sport.

Greg Bishop was last person at the *Times* who covered boxing in a meaningful way. At first, he was unfamiliar with the sport. But he was attracted to it, asked Tom Jolly if he could cover some fights, and became knowledgeable over time. Now that he's gone, the number of people on staff who are knowledgeable regarding and drawn to the sweet science can be expressed in arithmetic by a circle.

"There's a lot in boxing that speaks to the larger landscape in sports," Bishop recently told this writer. "PEDs, the role of the television networks, the lack of an effective governing body in contrast to how other sports are run. It was an uphill battle anytime I wanted to write about boxing at the *Times*. In the end, it was just ten percent of my time. But it was fun."

The *Times* sports section now features more longform journalism and offbeat topics than in the past. One hopes that, in the near future, its editors will realize that there are fascinating stories in boxing that go beyond mundane reporting on the outcome of fights and repetitious pro forma pieces on Floyd Mayweather and Manny Pacquiao.

The editors of the *New York Times* might not like the Tea Party, but they cover it. They should also cover boxing.

Floyd Mayweather's abusive conduct toward woman became an issue again in the days before his September 13, 2014, rematch against Marcos Maidana.

Floyd Mayweather and Ray Rice

Floyd Mayweather fought a rematch on Saturday night against Marcos Maidana at the MGM Grand in Las Vegas. Pre-fight tracking suggests that pay-per-view buys were disappointing and, once again, Showtime will lose millions of dollars on a Mayweather event.

But the ring action and pay-per-view numbers aren't the most important story surrounding Mayweather-Maidana II. Their first fight was contested on May 3, 2014 (four days after Floyd's foot-in-mouth comments regarding the racist remarks made by Los Angeles Clippers owner Donald Sterling). Mayweather-Maidana II was intertwined with another important social issue: violence against women.

Over the years, Mayweather has had significant issues with women and the criminal justice system. In 2002, he pled guilty to two counts of domestic violence. In 2004, he was found guilty on two counts of misdemeanor battery for assaulting two women in a Las Vegas nightclub. Then, on December 21, 2011, again in Las Vegas, Judge Melissa Saragosa sentenced Mayweather to ninety days in the Clark County Detention Center after he pled guilty to a battery domestic violence charge involving Josie Harris (the mother of three of his children) and no contest to two charges of harassment. According to the indictment, the battery domestic violence involved grabbing Harris by the hair, throwing her to the floor, striking her with his fist, and twisting her arm in front of two of the children. The harassment included threatening to kill Harris and her then-boyfriend or make her and the boyfriend "disappear." Mayweather served sixty-three days of his ninety-day sentence after receiving twenty-seven days off for good behavior.

More recently, on September 4 of this year, Shantel Jackson (Mayweather's former fiancée) filed suit against him in California, claiming that Floyd assaulted her shortly after his release from prison. The suit includes causes of action for assault, battery, false imprisonment, harassment, defamation, and the infliction of emotional distress. Jackson reminds some observers of Robin Givens. Her attorney is the equally likable Gloria Allred.

One of the many troubling aspects of Mayweather's conduct is the manner in which the powers that be have responded to it.

The Nevada State Athletic Commission didn't suspend Mayweather's license after he pled guilty to battery domestic violence. Judge Saragosa delayed the start of Floyd's jail term so he could fight Miguel Cotto on May 5, 2012. Golden Boy continued to promote his fights. And World Boxing Council president Jose Sulaiman declared, "Beating a lady is highly critical [but] it is not a major sin or crime."

HBO (which was televising Mayweather's fights on HBO-PPV at the time) aired a special in which Michael Eric Dyson (a professor at Georgetown University) interviewed Floyd and compared him with Muhammad Ali, Jim Brown, and Kareem Abdul-Jabbar as an oppressed black athlete that the system was trying to silence. The comparison with Brown seemed like the most appropriate of the three, given the fact that (despite an impressive record of community service and his status as possibly the greatest football player of all time), Brown once had the unfortunate habit of being physically abusive to women and, in one instance, threw a woman off a hotel balcony. But that awkward circumstance went unmentioned, as did the previous Mayweather convictions involving violence against women.

"Martin Luther King went to jail," Mayweather told Dyson. "Malcolm X went to jail. Am I guilty? Absolutely not. I took a plea. Sometimes they put us in a no-win situation to where you don't have no choice but to take a plea. I didn't want to bring my children to court."

Dyson then segued to the idea that there was a "racially-based resentment" against Mayweather and declared, "I think about Jay-Z on *Ninety-Nine Problems*, when he goes—the cop asks him a question, and he says—'Are you mad at me because I'm young, rich, and I'm famous and I'm black. Do you got a problem with that?'"

It's hard to escape the conclusion that Dyson's interview with Mayweather is another piece of the puzzle in the ongoing cycle of domestic violence against women, particularly in the African American community. And in the interest of equal time, it should be noted that Showtime (Mayweather's current home) has also been derelict in its response to Floyd's conduct toward women.

That brings us to former Baltimore Ravens running back Ray Rice.

Rice was arrested on February 15 of this year (and later indicted for third-degree aggravated assault) after punching his fiancée (now his wife) and knocking her unconscious in an elevator at the Revel Hotel and Casino in Atlantic City. Rice agreed to enter a pre-trial intervention program (which, if satisfactorily completed, would lead to dismissal of the criminal charges against him). On July 24, he was suspended for two games by National Football League commissioner Roger Goodell, who seemed intent on brushing the incident aside. Thereafter, Goodell was widely criticized for the leniency of the punishment. On August 28, he admitted that his response to the occurrence had been inadequate and announced that, henceforth, acts of domestic violence or sexual assault by NFL players or any other league personnel would be met by a six-game suspension with a second offense calling for a minimum suspension of one year.

Then, on September 8, TMZ posted a surveillance-camera video of the punch. Videos do more than confirm that an incident occurred. They have the potential to imprint the gruesome nature of a violent act on the consciousness of the nation. The public was already aware that Rice had punched his fiancée in an elevator. The video made it "real" and ignited a firestorm of outrage. That same day, Rice's contract was terminated by the Ravens and Goodell announced that Rice had been suspended by the NFL for a minimum of one year.

Then Mayweather had his say. On September 9, Floyd met with reporters after his "grand arrival" at the MGM Grand and was asked about Rice.

"I'm not here to say anything negative about him," Mayweather answered. "Things happen. You live and you learn. No one is perfect." Floyd also voiced the opinion. "They had said that they suspended him for two games. Whether they seen the tape or not, I truly believe that a person should stick to their word. If you tell me you're going to do something, do what you say you're going to do."

"Have you seen the video?" a reporter asked.

"Oh, yeah. I seen the video."

"It's kind of disturbing," the reporter pressed.

"I think there's a lot worse things that go on in other people's households also," Mayweather responded. "It's just not caught on video."

"I wish Ray Rice nothing but the best," Mayweather continued. "I know he's probably going through a lot right now because football is his passion. Football is his love. It's no different from me being in the fight game. If they told me, 'Floyd, you got the biggest deal in sports history' and a couple of months later they say, 'Your deal is taken away from you.' Oh, man. It's not really just the money; it's the love for the sport."

Then, further referencing his own history, Mayweather declared, "With my situation, no bumps, no bruises, no nothing. With O.J. and Nicole, you seen pictures. With Chris Brown and Rihanna, you seen pictures. With Ochocinco and Evelyn, you seen pictures. You guys have yet to see any pictures of a battered woman; a woman that claims she was kicked and beat [by me]."

Mayweather's comments elicited a strong response.

"It's impossible to hear that and not feel sick to your stomach," Greg Bishop of *Sports Illustrated* wrote. "The implication is enormous: *Other men beat their wives worse, so what's a woman in an elevator knocked out cold.* Mayweather will fight in another casino this weekend. The MGM Grand will host the proceedings. It's Mayweather plastered on the side of the hotel, his likeness stretching for dozens of stories above a sign that reads 'Home of the Champion.' Showtime Pay-Per-View will televise the bout. Hundreds of millions of dollars will be pocketed. It would be shocking if the same network and casino executives who opened their arms to Mayweather—and the money his fights produce—have not condemned Rice this week. Everybody has. But there's an obvious double-standard involved here, and one highlighted by Mayweather himself, in the one part of his comments that rang true. In Rice's case, there is a video. In most cases of domestic violence, there is not. The tangible evidence, the way anyone with a television or Internet connection can see Rice load up, swing his left fist, and crumple the woman he wanted to and did marry to the floor, somehow made it more real to the public. But it's not more real. It's just more visible, more visceral."

On September 9, reacting the outrage over his comments (and possibly, their potential to turn off would-be pay-per-view buyers), Mayweather issued a non-apologetic apology.

"If I offended anyone, I apologize," Mayweather said. "I didn't mean to offend anyone, and I apologize to the NFL and anyone else that got offended."

Maybe boxing fans should be thankful that Floyd didn't wear a Ray Rice jersey into the ring on Saturday night.

To repeat what I've written in the past: Somewhere in the United States tonight, a young man who thinks that Floyd Mayweather is a role model will beat up a woman. Maybe she'll walk away with nothing more than bruises and emotional scars. Maybe he'll kill her.

★ ★ ★

And a note from after the fight—

Warren Buffett has become one of the richest and most admired men in the world by researching fully before he invests and by standing on principle with regard to important issues. This past weekend, he did neither. Buffett attended the rematch between Floyd Mayweather and Marcos Maidana at the MGM Grand in Las Vegas and was interviewed in Mayweather's dressing room by Jim Gray of Showtime before the fight.

"It's a real thrill for me to be at a championship boxing match," Buffett said. "Never seen one in my life. I'm 84 years old, so it's about time."

Gray then asked Mayweather, "To have the credibility of this man means what to you?"

Mayweather responded. "You know; Warren Buffet, Bill Gates, Mark Cuban; those are the guys that, when I was young, I looked up to."

This followed an earlier visit by Buffett to the Mayweather Boxing Club in Las Vegas, after which Floyd referred to the founder of Berkshire Hathaway as "one of my billionaire friends."

Because of Buffett's record on social issues, one has to assume that he didn't understand the implications of his presence at Mayweather's side. He should have known better.

Boxing's literary tradition continued to grow in 2014

Literary Notes

Bouts of Mania by Richard Hoffer is keyed to five fights that are part of boxing lore: Ali-Frazier I, II, and III; Frazier-Foreman I; and Ali-Foreman. It's not a full recounting of the fighters' careers. Rather, it places these five fights in historical context and recreates certain scenes and moments that define the fights and the fighters themselves.

Three men, five fights, fifty-one rounds contested on four continents over fifty-five months.

In the end, Hoffer concedes, "the narrative would always belong to Ali." Madison Square Garden, Zaire, and Manila are now synonymous with historic fights. Jamaica (where Frazier and Foreman battled for the first time) isn't.

Still, Hoffer is on firm ground when he writes, "Pick any one of the three and he might have dominated boxing during a period when the game still mattered. He might have dominated the sports and celebrity culture that was then taking full bloom all on his own. But put them together? Three powerful and contrasting personalities, each a proxy for competing belief systems, each a highly visible (if not always willing) symbol for divided constituencies, and set them in pursuit of a single prize? The urgency, the sheer desperation of these men, produced a period of tumult never before seen, never seen again. Thrillas, Rumbles, Fights of the Century. A world sat ringside and gaped at their effort and determination (and nonsense, also) and wondered at these new and astounding levels of resolve. Somebody could get off a stool after that? Somebody could endure this and return for more? Wait, there's a trilogy in this madness?"

Boxing's most famous wars of attrition began with Ali-Frazier I at Madison Square Garden. That was when, in Hoffer's words, "Ali's hate crimes against Frazier" began.

"Ali," Hoffer writes, "was as much a poster boy for self-importance as he'd been a countercultural icon. But he was an accessible symbol for the revolution." As for Joe, Hoffer observes, "The idea that, just because Ali stood for something he must also, baffled Frazier. When did he pick sides? He'd never talked politics, race, or religion. How did he get involved in a national debate?"

Insofar as Joe was concerned, boxing was a fistfight between two men, nothing more and nothing less. It was "a straightforward activity, an honest acceptance of give-and-take. Frazier's frightening advantage," Hoffer contends, "was that he didn't particularly care how much he needed to take in order to give."

Frazier prevailed in Ali-Frazier I. Two years later, he journeyed to Jamaica to defend his throne against George Foreman.

Foreman wasn't looking forward to the prospect of combat against an adversary who was "like a boulder with a head."

"I want to be champ," George told himself. "But I don't want to fight him."

But as Hoffer notes, "Few events have the same capacity for surprise as a boxing match. Long-held values vacated, a bias corrected, the surety of opinion cancelled, a whole foundation of belief swallowed up in an instant. All in the time in takes a man to swing his arm."

Foreman knocked Frazier out in the second round. That relegated Ali-Frazier II (the least memorable of Hoffer's five fights) to regional-belt status. Then the fires began to rage brightly again.

"The fight crowd didn't particularly care where it was," Hoffer posits. "It was a movable mob, circulating here and there, reconvening at assigned sites, resuming old narratives. Location was of little consequence."

But Zaire, a nation under the boot of President Mobutu Sese Seko?

The Philippines, ruled with an iron fist by Ferdinand Marcos?

That led to moral ambiguities because, in Hoffer's words, "there wasn't another man in the world who could generate occasions for such useful propaganda." Ali had become "a symbol of independence that might be rented out and used to create new story lines for ambitious nations."

And then Hoffer asks the question, "Had Ali, whose physical and moral courage was a beacon through a dark and gloomy time, become nothing more than a hired hand, a troubadour of whatever politics paid the most, an advertisement of martial law?"

But those thoughts were far from the collective consciousness of boxing fans when Ali and Frazier met in Manila. One of the strengths of
Hoffer's writing is that the fight action itself is told with insight and drama.

Of Manila, Hoffer proclaims, "The fourteenth round—and it would
be the last one, the final three minutes of their shared agony—was a kind
of scientific experiment, an investigation into the extremes of human
behavior. Just exactly what was a person capable of? How far could he
go? How deep could he reach? Nobody had ever seen it conducted at
this level, precautionary measures usually in place that would abort any
further research, saving the subjects somewhere just short of death. So to
that extent, nobody really knew what desire and pride could accomplish,
or destroy. Now they did."

The final chapters of Hoffer's work bring the narrative up to the
present. Of the three warriors, it's Foreman who is healthy, wealthy, and,
even prior to Frazier's death, seemed to enjoy the happiest post-ring
years.

"Foreman alone among his blood brothers," Hoffer observes, "got
out alive." As for Ali and Frazier, "that's what happens when pride and
ambition become so inflamed that survival is no longer a part of the
game plan. Take a look, if you can."

"They made a bonfire of themselves," Hoffer concludes. "The
embers, after all this time, still smolder away."

★ ★ ★

Randy Roberts has written four books that are an important part of
boxing literature. The first had its origins in a doctoral dissertation about
Jack Dempsey that he wrote in the 1970s as a student at LSU.

"Very few people were writing seriously about sports history,"
Roberts says of that time. "I did my research. At one point, I went to
New York and interviewed Dempsey at his restaurant. He was in his
late-seventies by then and couldn't have been nicer. The first thing that
struck me was how big his hands were. They were enormous. When we
shook hands, my hand all but disappeared in his."

"We sat at the premier table in front of the restaurant, right by the
window," Roberts remembers. "People were constantly coming over to

shake Dempsey's hand and ask for an autograph. He was polite with everyone. He answered all of my questions, although I had the feeling that he'd been asked most of them many times before. Then his wife and step-daughter came in and he invited me to join them for dinner."

"I was a graduate student and a man of limited means," Roberts continues. Dempsey kept saying, "Have the steak. Have the cheesecake." Part of me was afraid that I'd end up washing dishes, but it was his treat. I was floating on air when I left the restaurant that night."

Roberts's dissertation, which was expanded and published as a book in 1979, is still the best of the Dempsey biographies. Four years later, he authored *Papa Jack: Jack Johnson and the Era of White Hopes*. That was followed by *Heavy Justice* (a study of Mike Tyson's rape trial, co-authored with prosecutor Greg Garrison) and *Joe Louis: Hard Times Man*.

At present, Roberts is researching a book that will focus on the years that Cassius Clay joined the Nation of Islam and evolved into Muhammad Ali. That leads to the question: "If Randy could spend a day with any of his five subjects—Johnson, Dempsey, Louis, Ali, Tyson—in their prime, which one would he choose?"

"That's a tough one," Roberts answers. "But the historian in me says Joe Louis. Because of his personality and the restrictions that were put upon him, Louis revealed the least of himself to the public. There was so much more to know about him than people knew. And the sad thing is that virtually none of it is retrievable anymore."

★ ★ ★

British boxing writer Bob Mee, who doubles as a commentator for Sky Sports, faced a problem while writing *A Tiger Rose out of Georgia*.

Tiger Flowers, who was born in rural Georgia and lived for much of his life in Atlanta, was the first black athlete to gain a widespread following among southern whites. In 1926, he added to his laurels by decisioning Harry Greb to become the first black middleweight champion of the world. Twenty-one months later, both Flowers and Greb were dead; the tragic consequence of "minor" surgeries gone wrong.

In 2012, after a long search, Mee tracked down Verna Lee Jackson (Flowers's only child). They spoke briefly on the telephone. Lee, then ninety years old, was living in Los Angeles. She told Mee that she'd talk with her family about whether or not to share her memories of her father. Then unrealistic financial demands were made and the interview never took place.

"It was very frustrating and disappointing," Mee recalls. "I don't know what Verna Lee could have added in terms of detailed firsthand information because she was so young when her father died. But she would have remembered something about him that would have added to the breadth of the story. And she and her mother appear to have lived together until the early 1940s, which means she would have heard her mother's stories about Flowers and their lives together."

Meanwhile, Mee writes of his subject, "Flowers built a bridge that led from Jack Johnson to Joe Louis, from the days when an African-American athlete was despised and whose success provoked anger and violence to the time when [after Louis defeated Max Schmeling in 1938] a man with African blood became the celebrated representative of the nation. Flowers would probably have laughed if anyone had suggested he had improved the way life was. But Louis was tolerated as his life began to take shape partly because of the example set by Flowers."

★ ★ ★

Confusing the Enemy: The Cus D'Amato Story by Scott Weiss and Paige Stover (Acanthus Publishing) is a massive book, weighing in at 729 pages and just under four pounds.

D'Amato was a complex man who attracted adjectives and nouns by the score. He was passionate, paranoid, elusive, enigmatic, controlling, charismatic, a genius with a brilliant boxing mind, and more. The authors write that he was deemed unfit for military service at the onset of World War II because a pre-induction examination determined that he had "great potential for leadership" but also "a high probability for psychiatric issues." For those who knew D'Amato, that rings true.

The book covers all of the familiar D'Amato touchstones such as his relationships with Floyd Patterson, Jose Torres, Mike Tyson, Jimmy Jacobs, and the mob.

There's also the claim that D'Amato was gay. A lot of people who knew Cus think that's true. The problem is that the contention is presented here in unsourced, often-novelized passages with fictitious dialogue.

That leads to the fundamental problem underlying *Confusing the Enemy*. The authors have chosen to present D'Amato's story through the eyes of a fictitious sportswriter named Mel Kunsterman, who appears in Zelig-like fashion throughout the book. This novelization means that it's hard for the reader to know what's fiction and what can be trusted as real. It also serves to cover up occasionally sloppy reporting and questionable statements of fact. For example, the authors maintain that D'Amato's training techniques enabled Jose Torres "to throw a six-punch combination in two-fifths of a second." I don't believe that's true.

In the end, *Confusing the Enemy* leaves its readers with an entertaining but flawed impressionistic portrait of a multifaceted man.

★ ★ ★

No Middle Ground by Sanjeev Shetty explores the five fights contested among Chris Eubank, Nigel Benn, and Michael Watson between June 21, 1989, and October 8, 1993. Eubank emerged with three wins and a draw. Watson's ledger was 1-1-1. Benn was knocked out by both men before earning a draw against Eubank.

The impact of the fights was magnified by the fact that they were seen in England by a mass audience on "free" television. They're best remembered for the horrifying drama of September 21, 1991. That night, going into the twelfth and final round, Watson was leading Eubank on all three judges' scorecards. But he was struggling badly, the result of bleeding in his brain.

The bout was stopped. Watson collapsed. He underwent multiple surgeries and was in a coma for forty days. Remarkably, he survived and regained many of his cognitive and physical functions. But he still suffers from impediments, including partial paralysis.

No Middle Ground paints a portrait of three fighters with diverse personalities labeled by the author as "a prancer [Eubank], a bully [Benn], and a straight man [Watson]."

Shetty writes honestly, saying, "Benn, Eubank, and Watson would probably only feature in the best-of category when the discussion turned to British boxers." And refreshingly, he acknowledges, "We all had our favorites. At times, we wanted one of them to win more than the other."

But Shetty's recitation of events is more workmanlike than soaring. And the best material in the book—his recounting of Watson's slow painful rehabilitation—is vague with regard to how things stand now.

That said; the message of *No Middle Ground* is clear. "Serious injury to boxers," Shetty writes, "is a permanent risk. And when you see it, you don't forget it."

★ ★ ★

Counterpunch (published by Triumph Books) is a collection of eighty-four columns that Ira Berkow wrote about boxing for the *New York Times* and Newspaper Enterprise Association between 1967 and 2005.

Berkow wrote with a nice, and sometimes cutting, touch. After Mike Tyson was knocked out by Buster Douglas, the scribe wondered if Iron Mike might henceforth refer to himself as "the second baddest man on the planet."

Writing about the star-studded crowd that attended the second fight between Joe Frazier and George Foreman, Berkow recounted, "Elizabeth Taylor was at ringside. She once held the title of Beauty Champion of the World, and she may still lay claim to it but not in very many states. She has had for years a problem with making the weight. There is a roundness to her face and a figure that could stand some roadwork."

Berkow also has an ear for good quotes. A few of my favorites are:

★ Jack Dempsey: "Some people still call me champ. I was champ 1919 to 1926. That's seven years. That's long enough. But they're nice people. You know, 'Hiya, champ. Hiya, champ' Still makes me feel good."

★ Joe Louis: "Jackie [Robinson] is my hero. He don't bite his tongue for nothing. I just don't have the guts, you might call it, to say what he says. And I don't talk so good either. That's for sure."

★ Trainer Whitey Bimstein (bemoaning the dwindling ranks of Jewish fighters): "Now that any kid can get a job, they got no ambition."

★ Jake LaMotta (while working as a bouncer in a strip club before *Raging Bull* turned his life around): "I love women, but I'm turned off here. You seen one topless broad, you seen 'em all."

★ British promoter Mickey Duff (referencing Larry Holmes just before Holmes fought Mike Tyson]: "Doesn't he look good? There are three ages of man: young, middle age, and doesn't he look good."

⋆ Roy "Cookie" Wallace (after being knocked down four times en route to a sixth-round stoppage at the hands of Bob Foster): "I got up from three knockdowns by the champ. Not many men can say that."

⋆ Andrew Golota (when it was pointed out that he had arrived for an eleven o'clock interview at 11:58): "But is still eleven."

⋆ Sandy Saddler (twelve years after retiring from boxing): "I'm fine and well off. You know it couldn't be any other way, because bad news travels fast and no one ain't heard nothing about me."

⋆ ⋆ ⋆

Hard Road to Glory is the autobiography of former WBO cruiser-weight titleholder and current Sky Sports commentator Johnny Nelson.

Nelson had only thirteen amateur contests, won three of them, lost his first three pro fights, and later endured a stretch where he come out on the losing end in seven of eleven bouts. There were times when, by his own admission, he was just going through the motions.

"I was out of love with boxing," he writes. "I didn't even watch videos of opponents. I was just a hooker, coldly doing the job and taking the money."

Nelson fought miserably in his first title opportunity (against Carlos DeLeon for the WBC belt in 1990). "From the moment I woke up on the morning of the fight," he admits, "I didn't want to go through with it."

Then the fight started, and Nelson recounts, "My boxing brain wasn't working. I backed off and threw nothing. I didn't blame people for being angry, especially those guys stuck in dead-end jobs who had shelled out good money in the expectation of seeing me take my chance to make something of myself, the kind of opportunity they could only dream about. [After the fight] I kept myself sane by reasoning that these people didn't know the real me. I found it harder to take when my family joined in the mass condemnation. That hurt because they did know me. Even my mother, who had watched the fight at home on television, said 'I couldn't believe it. Why didn't you hit him?'"

That's refreshingly honest writing.

And two years later, in a repeat of the DeLeon fiasco, Nelson admits that he stank out the joint in a challenge against IBF cruiserweight champion James Waring. After that bout, Sky TV commentator Glenn McCrory declared, "All you can put it down to is heart. He's scared. Every fighter has fear, especially in a big title fight. But that's something you have got to overcome. I don't think he'll ever do it now."

Promoter Frank Warren put things in perspective, saying, "If Johnny Nelson were fighting in my back garden, I would pull the curtains across [the window]."

But Nelson persevered. And his improbable journey turned golden in 1999, when he knocked out Carl Thompson to claim the WBO cruiser-weight crown. Fourteen successful title defenses (albeit against mediocre opposition) followed. Then, in 2006, Nelson snapped a patella tendon and his ring career was over.

Hard Road to Glory is an honest recounting of a fighter's life, in and out of the ring. I don't like the fact that boxing has more than a hundred variations of world champions in seventeen different weight divisions today. But Nelson comes across as so likable in the pages of his book that it's hard to begrudge him his belt.

How else can one feel about a fighter who, writing about former schoolmates and sparring partners, acknowledges, "There are a lot of people out there who still find it hard to believe I became champion of the world. They tell disbelieving children, 'I used to beat up Johnny Nelson.'"

★ ★ ★

The Gods of War by Springs Toledo is divided into three parts. The first consists of seven essays on boxing. The second (four essays) focuses on Sonny Liston (who Toledo suggests would have emerged triumphant from a round-robin tournament contested among the twenty-seven heavyweight champions from Jack Dempsey to the Klitschkos). These sections are followed by ten essays and supporting statistical data that lead to a ranking of the twenty "greatest fighters of the modern era."

Toledo is a gifted writer, and some of the inclusions in *The Gods of War* are very good. He starts with a quote from A. J. Liebling who, after souring on boxing, decided to journey to Indianapolis for the 1959 heavyweight title bout between Floyd Patterson and Brian London.

"I felt," Liebling wrote afterward, "the elation of a man who said a lot of hard things about a woman and is now on his way to make up."

Toledo also tells the tale of a heavyweight named Lonnie Craft (aka Battling Blackjack), who fought forty-one times between 1938 and 1954 and was executed in 1959 by the State of Arizona for first-degree murder.

"Craft," Toledo recounts, "walked to the gas chamber as if he were walking to the ring, wearing boxing gloves, shoes, trunks, and robe. An ex-fighter needed to feel brave one more time."

But then there are the rankings. Toledo evaluates fighters based on seven criteria: (1) quality of opposition, (2) ring generalship, (3) longevity, (4) dominance, (5) durability, (6) performance against larger opponents, and (7) intangibles. Based on these factors, he ranks Harry Greb as the greatest fighter of boxing's modern era.

A lot of knowledgeable boxing fans will have a problem with that. And they'll have a bigger problem with rankings that place Holman Williams in the top twenty while Sugar Ray Leonard and Carlos Monzon don't make the cut.

★ ★ ★

The Laughter of Strangers by Michael J. Seidlinger (Lazy Fascist Press) is a quirky novel.

Seidlinger tells the first-person story of Sugar Willem Floures (an aging fighter on the decline) through impressions, snippets, call them what you will. After reading fifty pages, I found myself saying, "This guy knows boxing. I like this book." Then, like a past-his-prime fighter struggling after some strong early rounds, the book implodes. Other readers might feel differently. I stopped caring about the characters and, eventually, I stopped reading.

That said . . . Seidlinger is an intriguing writer. So let me offer a sampling of the thoughts expressed in the early chapters of *The Laughter of Strangers*:

"Nothing is brighter than the lights shining on the ring on fight night . . . They watch the other guy, who does everything I do but maybe a little bit better . . . I had a chin. Cast-iron. Now I can hear glass shatter whenever I take one to the jaw . . . One of those straights that pushes through your gloves, causing your gloves to shoot back towards you and away, parting the sea as the powerful strike lands right on your nose. When it lands, there's little more than a tickle. It starts at the point of impact, the bridge of the nose. Feel it as it expands, impact warm. And the dots, they swarm your vision until you don't see much of anything. If you're lucky, you are still standing and fighting back. But lately I haven't been up on luck . . . Take a nap. The ring might as well have been a queen-sized bed. I was out cold."

"I'm going to keep applying pressure to the wound on my forehead and I'm not going to look in any mirrors . . . A rematch. What does it mean when I go pale, flush with fear, at such a thought? . . . The world might not care much longer. That's what bleeds the most, hurts the deepest. The thought that every punch landed, every punch absorbed, every scar carved into my skin, will be as insignificant as the dead buried six feet under. Some want infamy. Some want fame. Some fight. Some love. Some follow rather than lead. Everybody wants to be remembered . . . You probably already know what's going to happen. You know where this is going, right? . . . It is bad. I'm just not going to admit it until I have to . . . You know, but you don't understand."

Good writing; right?

Call this a strange review for a strange book.

The ritual "ten count" was a sad part of boxing in 2014.

In Memoriam

Jose Sulaiman, who built the World Boxing Council into a global empire, died in Los Angeles on January 16, 2014, at age eighty-two. He had undergone open-heart surgery at UCLA's Ronald Reagan Hospital on October 1, 2013, was in an intensive care unit for fifty days afterward, and never fully recovered.

Sulaiman was a master diplomat and a man of great personal charm. *The Guinness Book of Records* affirms that his thirty-eight-year reign as president of the WBC made him "the longest-serving president of a world sports organization."

Under Sulaiman's leadership, the WBC expanded to 161 member countries. To Jose's credit, he took a stand in the 1970s against the sanctioning of championship fights in apartheid South Africa. He also led the way in cutting world championship fights from fifteen to twelve rounds in a sincere effort to protect the health of fighters.

There were people, including members of Jose's family, who genuinely loved him. They have my sincere condolences. But it would be a disservice to history to not deal honestly with the whole of Sulaiman's legacy.

The WBC is officially designated as a not-for-profit corporation organized under Section 501(c)(6) of the Internal Revenue Code. It is not a charitable organization. But morally, if not legally, it is charged with a public trust.

It was widely understood throughout Sulaiman's tenure as president that the way to get what one wanted from the WBC was to massage Jose's ego and add to the WBC's coffers. He wasn't the only corrupting influence in boxing, but he was one of them.

It was never quite clear where the line was drawn between the WBC and Sulaiman's personal finances. One former member of the WBC board of governors (a successful businessman in his own right) observed, "There's no budget. There's no reserve fund. There's no money set aside for hard times and no financial accountability that I'm aware of. No matter how much we take in, there's never any money left at the end of the year. It's all spent, and that's very suspicious to me."

More notably, the WBC (like the other major world sanctioning organizations) was characterized by unconscionable rankings and a multiplicity of titles (world champions, interim champions, silver champions, champions emeritus) that ensured an endless stream of sanctioning fees but demeaned the sport.

Sulaiman's reign was also marked by the shameless attempt to deprive Buster Douglas of the WBC heavyweight title after he knocked out Mike Tyson in Tokyo; the appointment of judges who deprived Pernell Whitaker of victory over Julio Cesar Chavez; and the misappropriation of Sergio Martinez's crown in favor of Julio Cesar Chavez Jr.

These abuses and others like them didn't happen by accident. For each fighter, promoter, or manager who benefited from a Sulaiman favor, there were others whose dreams were crushed by his unsettling ways.

There was one historic moment of accountability. On March 21, 1998, Graciano Rocchigiani thought he had won the vacant WBC light-heavyweight championship by beating Michael Nunn. Then, after the fact, he was told that he had only fought for an "interim belt" and Roy Jones (who paid substantial sanctioning fees to the WBC by virtue of his multi-fight contract with HBO) was the real WBC champion.

Rocchigiani sued the WBC in federal court in the United States and won a $31,000,000 judgment. Sulaiman then threatened to take the WBC into bankruptcy and create a new sanctioning body unless the fighter accepted a lesser amount. That led writer Tim Graham to observe, "The WBC has filed for bankruptcy to avoid paying a $31 million court judgment. Just being morally bankrupt apparently wasn't good enough." Ultimately, the matter was settled with the WBC agreeing to pay $1,200,000 up front to Rocchigiani plus $300,000 a year for ten years.

Jose Sulaiman had a passion for boxing. It's sad when someone who has the potential to do so much good doesn't get the maximum good out of his powers. I wish he had listened to his better angels and used his remarkable skills to advance boxing in a more self-sacrificing way.

★ ★ ★

Something horrible happened on Valentines Day. Felix Figueroa died.

Felix was chief inspector for the New York State Athletic Commission. On fight night, inspectors are the eyes and ears of the commission in the dressing room and at ringside. Without inspectors, fight cards don't take place.

Felix was a good inspector and a calming presence amidst the chaos of fight night. His bilingual skills made him all the more valuable.

He was scheduled to work a fight card in Huntington, New York, on February 14, 2014. Late that morning, he telephoned fellow inspector George Ward and told him, "I'm not feeling good. I have a little shortness of breath. I think I'm coming down with a cold. Could you cover for me tonight?"

"Why don't you go to the hospital and get yourself checked out," Ward suggested.

Felix went to the hospital. The doctors found a coronary blockage. There was emergency surgery. He died on the operating table.

I saw Felix for the last time when he worked the fight card at Roseland on February 12. The New York State Athletic Commission is in a state of transition. The determination has been made that things aren't functioning the way they should. The governor's office has decided to create a new position: executive director. The executive director will be responsible for the day-to-day operation of the commission and play a role similar to that played by Marc Ratner, Keith Kizer, Larry Hazzard, and Greg Sirb in other states.

The New York secretary of state (which oversees the commission) has received many applications for the job. Some are from qualified applicants; others aren't. Some are from knowledgeable, well-intentioned people; others from hustlers and hacks.

Felix retired several years ago from his job as a station head for the United States Postal Service. That position spoke to his credentials. He was a sound administrator and understood how government agencies function. He had a good pension. He was enjoying his retirement. But the idea of serving as executive director for the commission intrigued him.

"I think I can make a difference," Felix told me in January. "There's so much they do at the commission that can be done better. If I came in, even if it was just for a year or two, I could turn things around and leave things better than when I found them. But before I do something like that, I'd have to talk with my family."

As I was leaving Roseland shortly before midnight on February 12, Felix approached me.

"Tommy," he said.

Felix and my aunt (who died several years ago) were the last two people who called me Tommy.

"I've been thinking some more about that job. Can we talk sometime next week?"

"Sure."

"I'll give you a call."

He was sixty-two years old.

George Ward served as an inspector with Felix for many years. George is one of the best.

"I'm struggling to come to grips with this," Ward said on Saturday morning. "Felix was a great guy. And he was a professional. He was always reliable. He always went the extra mile to help people out. He worked hard his entire life. This is horrible."

★ ★ ★

Monek Prager, the son of a rabbi, was born in Krakow, Poland, in 1929. In 1938, his family immigrated to England, where Monek became Mickey Duff. Between 1945 and 1949 (according to Boxrec.com), he engaged in 44 professional fights, compiling a record of 33 wins, 8 losses, and 3 draws.

"To say I couldn't punch wouldn't be accurate," Mickey told me once. "But I couldn't punch very hard."

He had four knockouts in those 44 fights.

Over time, Duff became one of England's premier matchmakers, managers, and promoters. He loved boxing and was a marvelous storyteller. One of his tales involved John Mugabi, the hard-punching junior-middleweight from Uganda.

"Early in John's career," Duff recalled, "I wanted to get him a fight in the United States. So I called Don King, and King matched him against

Curtis Ramsey in Atlantic City [on May 2, 1982]. I brought Mugabi over. Then an emergency came up and I had to go home. I hated to do it but there was no choice. All I could do was tell John's trainer, George Francis, to call with the result the minute the fight was over."

"So there I was, sitting in England, biting my nails when the phone rang," Duff continued. "It was George, telling me that Mugabi had knocked Ramsey out in the first round. Then Don King gets on the line and says, 'Mickey, the kid's good but we got a problem. He's begging me to take over his career. He says he wants Don King to promote him, but I told him no. I said you and I are friends, Mickey, and I won't take him on unless he lets me keep you as a fifty-fifty partner."

"Don," Duff countered "I didn't know you spoke Swahili."

"I don't," King responded.

"That's very interesting," Mickey said, "because Mugabi doesn't speak a word of English."

Duff had a way with words. Noting the mess that Hasim Rahman got himself into when he tried to avoid a contractually mandated rematch against Lennox Lewis, Mickey observed, "Rahman was three smart for his own good."

Speaking of a rival promoter, Duff said, "So many of his fighters wind up in the hospital, he should sell his limousine and buy an ambulance."

Commenting on the sad end of Muhammad Ali's career, Mickey opined, "Ali has nothing to be ashamed of. But the people who let him keep fighting do."

"The problem with boxing," he told me once, "is that common sense isn't common in boxing."

But the Mickey Duff declaration that stands foremost in my mind was a commentary on the sweet science. "There are no permanent friends in boxing," he declared. "And there are no permanent enemies in boxing."

Mickey Duff was a permanent friend. He died on Saturday (March 22, 2014) at the age of eighty-four. Boxing will miss him.

★ ★ ★

Jimmy Ellis (who died on May 6, 2014) was a good fighter and an honest man who had the dubious distinction of being one of boxing's first "alphabet-soup" champions.

Ellis turned pro as a middleweight in 1961 and worked his way up the ladder despite losing decisions to Holly Mims, Henry Hank, Rubin Carter, Don Fullmer, and George Benton. By 1967, he was a heavyweight. Then Muhammad Ali was stripped of his title for refusing induction into the United States Army. That paved the way for Ellis's participation in a World Boxing Association elimination tournament.

Victories over Leotis Martin, Oscar Bonavena, and Jerry Quarry followed. Ellis was now a beltholder, but there was no way the public would accept him as a champion. Any doubt on that score was put to rest on February 16, 1970, when Joe Frazier (who'd emerged as "New York State World Heavyweight Champion") unified the belts by knocking Jimmy unconscious in the fourth round.

Ellis retired from boxing in 1975 with 40 victories, 12 losses, and 1 draw. His final years were spent in a hellish dementia. History will remember him best for his relationship with Muhammad Ali.

Growing up in Louisville, Ellis and Ali (then known as Cassius Clay) were friends. They fought twice as amateurs, with each combatant winning once. From 1963 through 1967, Ellis was Ali's chief sparring partner. It was all but inevitable that they would meet in the ring "for real" someday. That moment came in the Houston Astrodome on July 26, 1971. It was Ali's first fight after losing to Joe Frazier in the "Fight of the Century." He knocked Ellis out in the twelfth round.

I interviewed Ellis in 1989 while researching *Muhammad Ali: His Life and Times*.

"I still love and respect the man," Ellis said of Ali. "Whatever he did, it came from the heart. He always treated me the way I wanted to be treated. I'm a Baptist. And no matter what was going on in his life, Ali never let religion come between us. From time to time, he talked to me about Islam. But I knew what I wanted to be, and he never pushed me to join his religion. Once, some of the guys in training camp pressured me about it. But Ali told them, 'Jimmy is my friend, and that's it. Whatever he wants to do is his business.'"

"The way I feel about Ali," Ellis continued, "he could call me any time of the day or night, I don't care where he'd be, and I'd be there for him. People worry now about his health. But there's a God. And it don't matter if his name is Jehovah or Allah. You can call him anything you want. God will look after Ali."

Now Ali will pray for Jimmy Ellis.

★ ★ ★

Zbigniew Pietrzykowski, who died in his native Poland on May 21, 2014, at the age of seventy-nine, had an illustrious amateur career. He won gold medals at the European Amateur Boxing championships in 1955, 1957, 1959, and 1963 and bronze medals at the Olympics in 1956 and 1964. But he's best known for a fight that was contested at the Rome Olympics on September 5, 1960. That day, Pietrzykowski lost in the gold-medal round to an eighteen-year-old American named Cassius Marcellus Clay Jr.

Clay had won his first three bouts in the 178-pound division. But in the first round against Pietrzykowski, he seemed a bit intimidated by his opponent's physical strength and confused by the Pole's southpaw style. Pietrzykowski outlanded him by a 16-to-11 margin.

Then, in round two, Clay established his jab and began scoring with sharp right hands for a 15-to-11 edge. By round three, he'd figured Pietrzykowski out and outlanded his foe 28 to 9, leaving the Pole dazed and bloodied at the final bell for a unanimous-decision triumph.

Pietrzykowski never turned pro. But in a sense, Muhammad Ali's later victories became his own. Decades later, the Polish fighter reminisced about those three rounds at the Rome Olympics and declared, "During the fight itself, I had to work at a very fast pace to avoid his punches. This was good for the first round. Clay was missing a lot of punches. But in the second round, I realized I was losing my strength and that it would be difficult for me to survive three rounds. I had to think about defense, and that hampered thoughts of victory. It left me with nothing else but to try to survive three rounds and not be knocked out. I would have done anything then to beat him. But later, I began to cherish his victories."

★ ★ ★

Former light-heavyweight champion Matthew Saad Muhammad died on May 25, 2014, at the much-too-young age of fifty-nine.

Saad Muhammad came from hard surroundings. His mother died when he was an infant. The aunt charged with raising him abandoned

Matthew when he was five. Police found him wandering along a Philadelphia highway. He was raised by foster parents as "Matthew Franklin" and later changed his name to Matthew Saad Muhammad.

Saad Muhammad fought like a 175-pound Arturo Gatti. And he did it in an era when the light-heavyweight division was particularly deep. His wars against a succession of top opponents highlighted by a twenty-eight-month reign as WBC champion became part of the consciousness of a generation.

Saad Muhammad dealt out beatings and he absorbed them. He was always willing to go in tough. In the glory years, he defeated Marvin Johnson, Yaqui Lopez, and John Conteh twice each and suffered losses at the hands of Dwight Muhammad Qawi (twice) and Eddie Mustafa Muhammad. Thirteen losses on the downside of his career dropped his final record to 49 victories against 16 defeats with 3 draws.

Seven years ago, I had occasion to talk with Saad Muhammad about the first professional fight he ever saw. His recollection of that night offers a clue as to his fighting style.

"It was at the Blue Horizon in Philadelphia," Saad Muhammad told me. "I was seventeen years old. My amateur coach took me. The fighters were punishing each other like rock 'em sock 'em robots. It was like Hollywood. No normal man could take that kind of punishment. But they had victory in their eyes, and I could see that the desire to win lessened the pain they felt. My coach said to me, 'This is what it's going to be like if you turn pro. To win, you'll have to condition yourself physically and mentally. Do you think you can do this?' And I told him, 'Whatever it takes, I'm going to do this. I can take the punishment. I can take the pain.'"

★ ★ ★

James Garner, who died on July 19, 2014, at age eighty-six, was an American icon. He rose to fame during the golden age of television in the role of Bret Maverick (an amiable gambler in the old American west). Later, he starred as detective Jim Rockford in *The Rockford Files*. His credits included more than fifty feature films highlighted by lead roles in *The Great Escape, 36 Hours,* and *The Americanization of Emily*. He was a good actor.

I met Garner at a dinner in 1993. The Smithsonian Institution was honoring five great athletes—Muhammad Ali, Arnold Palmer, Kareem Abdul-Jabbar, Chris Evert, and Ted Williams—who had helped shape America. The two-day program included a White House reception, a formal dinner, and an awards ceremony, which was taped for television and attended by Bill Clinton. I was invited by virtue of having been the authorized biographer for both Ali and Palmer. Garner (who was friends with Arnold) was there at Palmer's invitation.

Palmer introduced us.

Garner had played football and basketball in high school and appreciated athletic greatness. I told him how much I'd enjoyed *Maverick* when I was growing up, which I'm sure people told him fifty times a day. He was gracious and friendly. But what I remember best about the moment was Garner saying, "I'm just a guy who reads lines that someone else wrote. This man [putting his arm around Palmer] is special."

Then Garner pointed across the room to where Ali was standing and said, "That man is beyond special."

James Garner made life a lot more entertaining and fun for the rest of us. He was special.

★ ★ ★

As the number of boxing websites grows exponentially each year, the number of print magazines devoted to the sweet science grows smaller. For almost a century, *The Ring* has been the preeminent boxing publication in the United States. In the United Kingdom, it has shared honors for the past quarter-century with *Boxing Monthly*.

Boxing Monthly owed much of its success to its editor, Glyn Leach. Glyn cared deeply about boxing and understood it well. He was also the sort of editor that writers love to work with. Pitch an article idea to him, and you got a quick "yes" or "no" in response. He respected his writers' words and involved them in the editing process.

Leach died suddenly on August 17, 2014, at age fifty-two. He will be missed, by boxing and by everyone who wrote for him.

★ ★ ★

A unique figure in the world of boxing passed into history on September 1, 2014, when Charlie Powell died.

Powell starred in football, basketball, baseball, and track at San Diego High School. After graduation, he signed a contract with the St. Louis Browns, intent on making the major leagues. But he gave up baseball after one season to join the San Francisco 49ers in the National Football League.

Powell played five seasons as a defensive end with the 49ers (1952–1953 and 1955–1957) and two more with the Oakland Raiders in the fledgling American Football League (1960–1961). He also boxed.

Powell was a serious fighter. This wasn't a Mark Gastineau or Ed "Too Tall" Jones type of foray. His first pro fight was a draw against Fred Taylor on March 7, 1953. Then he returned to the gridiron. But football players were paid poorly in the 1950s. The average NFL player made less than $10,000 a season. So after the 1953 campaign, Powell decided to concentrate on boxing. He fought fourteen times over the next sixteen months before rejoining the 49ers in autumn 1955. He also sat out the 1958 and 1959 seasons to concentrate on the sweet science.

Powell suffered from poor management during his ring career. In big fights, he was always the opponent. Also, as he told Earl Gustkey of the *Los Angeles Times* in 2000, "A lot of people told me I was making a mistake playing in the NFL. And they were right in the sense that you don't need the same muscles in boxing you use in football."

Still, Powell rose as high as #4 in *The Ring's* heavyweight rankings. The high point of his fistic career came on March 4, 1959, when he knocked out Nino Valdes (then the second-ranked heavyweight in the world) in eight rounds.

But Powell's most memorable night in boxing came on January 24, 1964, when he fought a 16-and-0 heavyweight named Cassius Marcellus Clay Jr.

Clay was coming off a fourth-round knockout of Archie Moore and was attracting national media attention, although there were doubts that he would ever be an elite fighter.

Mort Sharnik, who covered Clay-Powell for *Sports Illustrated*, attended the pre-fight weigh-in and told this writer, "As usual Cassius was talking all that jive, making predictions, and doing routines with his greeting-card poetry. He was very imaginative and he was talking about Powell as if he were a child fantasizing. You know, 'I'll do this to that old monster; he's Frankenstein; I'll turn him inside out.' And that's fine until you meet Frankenstein. Now he was face-to-face with Charlie Powell at the weigh-in. Powell was very big, very strong, much more muscular than Clay. Cassius looked at him and, all of a sudden, a touch of reality began to creep in. They started rapping at one another. Cassius seemed a little apprehensive. Powell's brother, Art, who was a football player; he was there, and he's a talker too. Finally, Cassius got really agitated. He'd taken his shirt off for the weigh-in, his undershirt, and then he put it back on backwards, which of course Powell pointed out. So Clay fumed and fussed and announced, 'I'm going,' and he opened the door and stomped into a broom closet."

But fight night belong to Clay. He knocked Powell out in the third round.

"When he first hit me," Powell said afterward, "I thought to myself, I can take two of those to get in one of my own. But in a little while, I found out I was getting dizzier and dizzier every time he hit me, and he hurt. Clay throws punches so easily you don't realize how much they shock you until it's too late."

Meanwhile, Sharnik had an epiphany of his own.

"It was at that fight," he later recounted, "that I recognized Clay was an extraordinary fighter. In the second round, Powell hit him a shot to the solar plexus, a right hand underneath and a left hand on top. The shot to the solar plexus sunk in, it seemed, up to his elbow. Clay was hurt, but he controlled everything. Outside of that grunt, that oomph, when a man is hit—and physically, you can't do anything about that; it's compression of air—outside of that, you saw nothing. He sagged for a split second, but there was no change in his facial muscles. And when Powell went to follow up, Clay incredibly just fired back. Before the round was over, he had Powell cut over the eye, and he stopped him one round later."

Powell retired from boxing in 1965 with a record of 25 wins, 11 losses, and 3 draws with 17 knockouts. In his final years, he suffered from dementia. The combination of football and boxing had taken a toll. But no player in NFL history was a better fighter.

★ ★ ★

When Dan Goossen telephoned, he would announce himself in a unique way. There was no "Hi, Tom" or "This is Dan." Just . . .

"Aaaaaayyy !!!"

One time, I told him that he sounded like a beached whale.

"The whale is a noble mammal," Dan responded.

I liked Dan. His death this morning [September 29, 2014) from complications caused by liver cancer at age sixty-four came as a shock. It's unsettling when someone you've known as a healthy vibrant person dies suddenly from natural causes. And that's particularly true in Dan's case since he was such a strong, physically imposing presence.

Larry Merchant once said, "I like boxing people, and I like being one of them."

Dan was a boxing guy. His father was a Los Angeles cop, who later became a private detective. In 1982, Dan and his siblings started Ten Goose Boxing (named for Dan, his two sisters, and seven brothers) to train and manage fighters.

"Our first gym was the backyard of my brother Greg's house," Dan later recalled. "We had a speed-bag and heavy-bag hanging from a tree. One of the ring posts was on top of what had once been home plate for our family whiffle-ball games. Every morning, I'd sweep leaves out of the ring."

Eventually, Ten Goose received a waiver from the California State Athletic Commission that allowed it to simultaneously promote and manage fighters. In 1996, Dan and Mat Tinley (who had sold international television rights for Ten Goose) formed America Presents. In 2002, Dan and Ronald Tutor joined forces to form Goossen Tutor Promotions.

At one point, Goossen was also the promoter of record for Mike Tyson. But it was an unhappy experience.

"Signing Mike Tyson was the worst deal I ever made," Dan told me over drinks one night at the Parker Meridien Hotel in New York. "I've had to become somewhat indifferent to Mike's conduct in order to survive emotionally. And financially, it hasn't been a very good deal either. We get a fixed sum for each fight. The problem is, we're Mike's promoter of record, but basically all we are is a salaried name entity. The deal doesn't allow us to be promoters. We're not part of the decision-making process. There are a lot of things I'd do differently if we were really his promoter, but, in truth, we're not. There's nothing worse than being a passenger in a car and getting lost when you know that, if you were driving, you'd get to your destination. I don't like being relegated to the role of hanging up banners at press conferences. But the way the deal is structured, we aren't the ones who are directing the athlete."

Dan loved the sport and business of boxing and he loved the action. He never quite made it to the top rung. David Tua and Chris Arreola (two of his fighters) had heavyweight championship fights but fell short of boxing's ultimate prize. Andre Ward ascended to the number two slot on many pound-for-pound lists, but seemed to forget Dan's role in getting him to where he was.

Now the remembrances are flowing in. One of them comes from Seth Abraham, who was the architect and master builder of HBO Sports.

In mid-2000 (Abraham's last year at the network), he and Goossen had a heated disagreement that stemmed from Dan withholding what Seth felt was important information about the physical condition of one of Dan's fighters who was scheduled to appear on HBO. When the two men met at Abraham's office, Seth refused to shake hands, saying, "Let's just do our business and not pretend." Dan responded, "If you won't shake my hand, we have no business to discuss." Abraham said that he'd decide whether or not to shake hands after the meeting, and Goossen told him that the meeting was over.

"I was wrong," Abraham said this morning as he reminisced about Goossen. "The only fights that HBO's subscribers care about are the fights in the ring. So I made arrangements soon afterward to have coffee with Dan at The Palace Hotel. We met. I shook his hand. And as part of our conversation, I told him, 'You know; Don King and I have had many heated disagreements over the years. But one thing Don understands is that, when you have bad news to deliver, you do it promptly and directly.'"

Goossen thought for a moment and responded, "I know you're being serious with me, because no one has ever compared me unfavorably with Don King before."

* * *

Ernie Terrell was a nice man with a gentle way about him. He fought professionally for sixteen years, and finished his ring career with a

48-and-9 record. That included victories over Cleveland Williams, Zora Folley, Bob Foster, Eddie Machon, George Chuvalo, and Doug Jones. But Terrell is best remembered for three words: "What's my name!"

On February 6, 1967, Terrell fought Muhammad Ali at the Astrodome in Houston. It was a brutal ugly fight. During the promotional build-up to the bout, Terrell had referred to Ali as "Clay." That set the stage for what followed.

In the early rounds, Terrell suffered a fractured bone under his left eye and swelling of the left retina. By the middle rounds, he was virtually helpless. From that point on, Ali taunted him mercilessly. Time and again, he shouted, "What's my name," followed by a burst of blows to Terrell's eyes. "Uncle Tom! What's my name! Uncle Tom! What's my name!"

By the fourteenth round," Tex Maule later wrote, "Terrell could no longer control his tormented body. Instead of reacting normally to a feint, he flinched instinctively with his whole being. When he ventured to lead with his left, his recovery into a protective crouch was exaggerated and pitiful. It was a wonderful demonstration of boxing skill by Ali and a barbarous display of cruelty."

The scoring was 148–137, 148–137, 148–133 in Ali's favor.

"People ask me how I feel about that fight," Terrell told me years later. "They're interested in Ali's talking to me. But to be honest, I didn't hear him saying, 'What's my name.' I had other things I was worrying about. He might have said it, but I wasn't concentrating on stuff like that. I wasn't listening to him that night. I was busy trying to survive."

Terrell suffered from dementia in his later years and died on December 16, 2014, at age seventy-five. It's sad that he will be best remembered for the ugliest night of his life.

As 2014 progressed, the underside of the Floyd Mayweather saga became increasingly apparent.

Floyd Mayweather, Showtime, and the Nevada State Athletic Commission

Les Moonves has a domestic violence problem. As president and CEO of CBS Corporation, he oversees a vast media empire that includes, among other properties, CBS and Showtime.

CBS is one of the networks that televises National Football League games. The burgeoning NFL domestic violence scandal isn't adversely affecting ratings right now. But there might come a time when corporate advertisers move away from the NFL. That would be bad for CBS.

Meanwhile, Showtime finds itself joined at the hip with Floyd Mayweather by virtue of a six-fight contract. Mayweather has been criminally convicted on three separate occasions for being physically abusive to women. In 2012, he served sixty-three days in jail for one of these offenses. The Nevada State Athletic Commission didn't suspend Mayweather's license to box after any of the convictions, and the sentencing judge delayed the start of Mayweather's jail term so he could fight Miguel Cotto in Las Vegas on May 5, 2012.

Let's put that in perspective. Suppose Seattle Seahawks quarterback Russell Wilson (an exemplary citizen by all accounts) had been convicted of battery domestic violence and sentenced to prison last year. And suppose the sentencing judge had deferred sentence so Wilson could play against the Denver Broncos in the Super Bowl before going to jail. And suppose NFL commissioner Roger Goodell had let Wilson play. That's the equivalent of what happened with Mayweather in Nevada.

This week, the Mayweather, Showtime, and Nevada State Athletic Commission pathologies collided.

Showtime prides itself on its *All Access* series that the Showtime website describes as follows: "This documentary series from Emmy-Award-winning Showtime Sports provides viewers with an intimate portrait of some of the most compelling personalities in sports. *All Access* will take you inside the personal lives of the fighters and behind the scenes of the provocative and often edgy world of boxing with unrestricted access, as only Showtime can."

As part of the pre-event promotion for the September 13, 2014, pay-per-view fight between Mayweather and Marcos Maidana, Showtime aired a three-part *All Access* documentary. During the second episode, Sharif Rahman (an amateur boxer and one of former heavyweight champion Hasim Rahman's sons) was shown taking a vicious beating at the hands of Donovan Cameron in a sparring session at the Mayweather Boxing Club. Sharif's older brother, Hasim Rahman Jr, then challenged Cameron to get into the ring with him. The *All Access* documentary showed members of the gym placing bets on the action, while the two men fought for thirty-one consecutive minutes until Cameron could no longer continue. Mayweather cheered enthusiastically during the battle and said on camera, "The dog house; the rules are you fight till whoever quits. Guys fight to the death. It's not right, but it's dog house rules."

In the same episode of *All Access*, Mayweather was shown at home, watching as several women rolled joints and smoked marijuana. At one point, he instructed a third party to go to the store and buy more rolling paper because they had run out of paper.

Thereafter, Nevada State Athletic Commission chairman Francisco Aguilar told ESPN.com, "I watched the episodes when they were sent to me by another commissioner. Our main concern is the health and safety of the fighters, and not just on fight night but also in sparring and in training. We want to get a clarification about what happened on *All Access*. There were situations in sparring sessions that we need to talk about. One thing is to talk about making sure you have two equally paired fighters and that you're not putting one fighter in danger. The other is the round that went 31 minutes. There is also the marijuana situation in there, and some commissioners are upset about it."

On September 18, 2014, the Nevada State Athletic Commission instructed Mayweather to appear at its September 23 meeting to answer questions regarding the content of the *All Access* episode. He was not required to take an oath before testifying. That created a loophole through which, were he so inclined, he could testify falsely without exposure to prosecution for perjury.

Mayweather told the commission on September 23 that, contrary to what was represented on *All Access*, there had been three or four breaks during the thirty-one-minute round and that the marijuana shown in the documentary wasn't real marijuana but a prop used to engender interest in his lifestyle and help sell pay-per-view buys.

It's hard to believe that Showtime would stage events like that for inclusion in a documentary. The network is part of a media empire that includes CBS, perhaps the world's most respected name in news coverage.

Mayweather had an "executive producer" credit for *All Access*, but his reputation isn't on the line. The other three executive producers were Ross Greenburg, Jody Heaps, and Jason Bowers. Bowers was also credited as the series director. The prevailing view among industry insiders is that these men have too much integrity to stage scenes in the manner testified to by Mayweather.

Moreover, multiple sources at Showtime have told this writer that Mayweather's testimony before the Nevada State Athletic Commission was false.

"As you can imagine, it's a sensitive time right now," one of these sources said. "People here are angry. The marijuana was real. There was no break in the thirty-one-minute fight. Floyd flat out lied to the commission."

To date, Showtime executives have declined to comment publicly on Mayweather's testimony. But this is an instance where "no comment" is an inadequate response. The network owes its subscribers and the viewing public a clarification. Either the *All Access* scenes were genuine or they were not. That means it's incumbent upon Showtime management to call in key production personnel, ask them precisely what happened, and review all relevant video evidence. Then Showtime should either (1) apologize publicly for deliberately misleading its subscribers and the general public or (2) state publicly that, upon review, it has confirmed that the *All Access* presentation of events was accurate.

Meanwhile, the Nevada State Athletic Commission should also follow up on the matter. At a minimum, this would involve (1) requiring Mayweather and the appropriate Showtime personnel to testify under oath, and (2) requesting that subpoenas be issued for all relevant video content.

NSAC executive director Bob Bennett is a former FBI agent. He knows how to investigate something of this nature. And because Bennett is a former FBI agent, the commission will look pretty silly if it comes to light later on that its members were lied to and did nothing about it.

It's one thing if the Nevada State Athletic Commission accommodates Mayweather by allowing him to fight Miguel Cotto after he has pled guilty to battery domestic violence but not yet served his sentence. That's a choice, however unfortunate, that the NSAC made freely and knowingly. It's a very different matter if Mayweather has disrespected the commission and made a mockery of its proceedings by lying to the commissioners.

The credibility of both the Nevada State Athletic Commission and Showtime is at stake. If Mayweather told the truth at the September 23 hearing, then heads should roll at Showtime. If it was Mayweather who lied, it's time for the NSAC to say, "Enough is enough!" That would include re-examining Mayweather's license as a boxer and also the issue of whether Mayweather Promotions is fit to be licensed as a promoter in Nevada.

One assumes that Nevada governor Brian Sandoval (who bears ultimate responsibility for the commission and its actions) will be watching. So will Les Moonves. Either Showtime has deliberately deceived its subscribers and the general public or the five commissioners of the Nevada State Athletic Commission have been played for fools.

DISCARD